Las Vegas
2009

*A Selection
of **Restaurants** & **Hotels***

G936L.
6 M 58)
2009

Manufacture française des pneumatiques Michelin
Société en commandite par actions au capital de 304 000 000 EUR
Place des Carmes-Déchaux – 63000 Clermont-Ferrand (France)
R.C.S. Clermont-Fd B 855 200 507

Dépot légal Octobre 2008

Made in Canada

Published in 2008

Cover photograph : Getty Images / George Doyle

Although the information in this guide was believed by the authors and publisher
to be accurate and current at the time of publication, they cannot accept
responsibility for any inconvenience, loss, or injury sustained by any person relying
on information or advice contained in this guide. Things change over time and
travelers should take steps to verify and confirm information, especially time-
sensitive information related to prices, hours of operation, and availability.

Please send your comments to:
Michelin Maps & Guides
One Parkway South
Greenville, SC 29615 USA
Michelinguide.com
Michelin.guides@us.michelin.com

Dear reader

*W*e are thrilled to launch the second edition of our Michelin Guide Las Vegas.

Our teams have made every effort to produce a selection that fully reflects the rich diversity of the restaurant and hotel scene in the Neon Jungle.

The Michelin Guide provides a comprehensive selection and rating, in all categories of comfort and prices. As part of our meticulous and highly confidential evaluation process, Michelin's American inspectors conducted anonymous visits to restaurants and hotels in Las Vegas. Our inspectors are the eyes and ears of the customers, and thus their anonymity is key to ensure that they receive the same treatment as any other guest. The decision to award a star is a collective one, based on the consensus of all inspectors who have visited a particular establishment.

Our company's two founders, Édouard and André Michelin, published the first Michelin Guide in 1900, to provide motorists with practical information about where they could service and repair their cars, and find quality accommodations and a good meal. The star-rating system for outstanding restaurants was introduced in 1926. The same system is used for our American selections.

We sincerely hope that the Michelin Guide Las Vegas 2009 will become your favorite guide to the area's restaurants and hotels.

The Michelin Guide

"This volume was created at the turn of the century and will last at least as long".

This foreword to the very first edition of the MICHELIN Guide, written in 1900, has become famous over the years and the Guide has lived up to the prediction. It is read across the world and the key to its popularity is the consistency in its commitment to its readers, which is based on the following promises.

→ Anonymous Inspections

Our inspectors make anonymous visits to hotels and restaurants to gauge the quality offered to the ordinary customer. They pay their own bill and make no indication of their presence. These visits are supplemented by comprehensive monitoring of information—our readers' comments are one valuable source, and are always taken into consideration.

→ Independence

Our choice of establishments is a completely independent one, made for the benefit of our readers alone. Decisions are discussed by the inspectors and the editor, with the most important decided at the global level. Inclusion in the guide is always free of charge.

→ The Selection

The Guide offers a selection of the best hotels and restaurants in each category of comfort and price. Inclusion in the guides is a commendable award in itself, and defines the establishment among the "best of the best."

How the MICHELIN Guide Works

➔ Annual Updates

All practical information, the classifications, and awards, are revised and updated every year to ensure the most reliable information possible.

➔ Consistency & Classifications

The criteria for the classifications are the same in all countries covered by the Michelin Guides. Our system is used worldwide and is easy to apply when choosing a restaurant or hotel.

➔ The Classifications

We classify our establishments using 𝕏𝕏𝕏𝕏-𝕏 and 🏨🏨🏨-🏠 to indicate the level of comfort. The ✿✿✿-✿ specifically designates an award for cuisine, unique from the classification. For hotels and restaurants, a symbol in red suggests a particularly charming spot with unique décor or ambiance.

➔ Our Aim

As part of Michelin's ongoing commitment to improving travel and mobility, we do everything possible to make vacations and eating out a pleasure.

The Michelin Guide

Contents

To locate restaurants in selected Strip resorts, refer to floorplans in the "Where to stay" section.

Contents

How to use this guide

Where to **eat**

Restaurant Classifications by Comfort

More pleasant if in red

X	Quite comfortable
XX	Comfortable
XXX	Very comfortable
XXXX	Top class comfortable
XXXXX	Luxury in the traditional style

The Michelin Distinctions for good cuisine

Stars for good cuisine

✿✿✿	Exceptional cuisine, worth a special journey
✿✿	Excellent cuisine, worth a detour
✿	Very good cuisine in its category

Map Coordinates

Lucky Wrenn's (Starlight)

Gastropub X

A2 144555 E. Photographers Drive (at Peter Ln.)

Lunch & dinner daily

Phone: 702-345-9999
Web: www.luckywrenns.com
Prices: $

Styled like an English pub, Lucky Wrenn's is the perfect place to stop for a pint after a day at the gambling tables. Dark wood paneling, burgundy leather banquettes, and a boisterous bar area set the scene for an off-Strip party any night of the week.

Locals pack this place for both lunch and dinner. The reason will be clear once you dig into a filling fare like the tasty steak and kidney pie topped with a flaky whole-wheat crust. It's not unusual to see some of the city's top chefs here noshing at the bar late at night; the place enjoys a loyal following among the area's culinary professionals.

In traditional tavern style, Lucky Wrenn's offers its own house brew as well as a back room equipped with dart boards and a pool table for some old-fashioned gaming fun. Sure, it's not black jack, but if you're not careful, you could still lose some money here.

Sonya's Palace ✿✿✿

Italian X

B3 100 Reuther Place (at Sasha Blvd.)

Phone: 702-867-5309
Web: www.sonyasfabulouspalace.com
Prices: $$$$

Home cooked Italian never tasted so good unpretentious little place. The simple décor c name designers, and while the Murano glass lig chic and the velveteen-covered chairs are co isn't a restaurant where millions of dollars we interior.

Instead, food is the focus here. The restaurant' be Italian, but it nonetheless serves some of t the city, made fresh in-house. Dishes follow t ravioli may be stuffed with fresh ricotta and le and pumpkin in fall. Most everything is libe Parmigiano Reggiano, a favorite ingredient e

For dessert, you'll have to deliberate betw creamy tiramisu, ricotta cheesecake, and h One thing's for sure: you'll never miss you when you eat at Sonya's.

Appetizers	Entrées
• Crostini alla Toscana	• Lasagna Bolognese
• Antipasti della Casa	• Gnocchi alla Sorrentina
• Funghi con Polenta	• Grilled Lamb Chops "Scotta Dita"

152

Restaurant Symbols

🃏	Cash only
♿	Wheelchair access
🍴	Garden or terrace dining
🍳	Brunch
🍷	A particularly interesting wine list
🚗	Valet parking
🍽	Late dining

Price Classification

∞	under $25
$$	$25 to $50
$$$	$50 to $75
$$$$	over $75

Las Vegas areas

Each area is color coded...

■ The Strip
■ East Of The Strip
■ West of the Strip
■ Downtown

How to use this guide

West of The Strip

8

Where to **stay**

Average Prices

Prices do not include applicable taxes

$	under $150
$$	$150 to $250
$$$	$250 to $350
$$$$	over $350

Map Coordinates

Hotel Symbols

149 rooms	No of rooms and suites
♿	Wheelchair access
🏋	Exercise room
🌀	Spa
🏊	Swimming pool
🍽	Buffet
🐾	Pet Friendly

Hotel Classifications by Comfort

More pleasant if in red

🏠	Quite comfortable
🏠	Comfortable
🏠	Very comfortable
🏠	Top class comfortable
🏠	Luxury in the traditional style

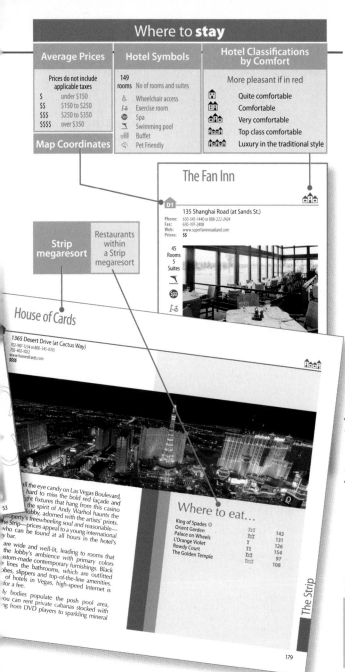

The Fan Inn

D1

135 Shanghai Road (at Sands St.)

Phone: 650-345-1440 or 888-222-2424
Fax: 650-397-2408
Web: www.superfaninnoakland.com
Prices: $$

45 Rooms
5 Suites

🏊 🌀 🏋

Strip megaresort

Restaurants within a Strip megaresort

House of Cards

1365 Desert Drive (at Cactus Way)
702-987-1234 or 800-345-8765
702-402-3022
www.houseofcards.com
$$$$

...all the eye candy on Las Vegas Boulevard,
...hard to miss the bold red façade and
...ght fixtures that hang from this casino
...the spirit of Andy Warhol haunts the
...lobby, adorned with the artists' prints.
...the property's freewheeling soul and reasonable—
...the Strip—prices appeal to a young international
...who can be found at all hours in the hotel's
...y bar.

...are wide and well-lit, leading to rooms that
...the lobby's ambience with primary colors
...ustom-made contemporary furnishings. Black
...e lines the bathrooms, which are outfitted
...obes, slippers and top-of-the-line amenities.
...of hotels in Vegas, high-speed Internet is
...for a fee.

...ly bodies populate the posh pool area,
...ou can rent private cabanas stocked with
...g from DVD players to sparkling mineral

Where to eat...

King of Spades ☺		
Orient Garden	XxX	143
Palace on Wheels	XxX	131
L'Orange Violet	X	126
Rowdy Court	XX	154
The Golden Temple	XxY	97
	XYxY	108

The Strip

How to use this guide

179

9

A brief history of Las Vegas

America's fastest growing metro area, Las Vegas, claimed just over 39 million visitors in 2007. Whether they come here to shop, be entertained, or just to gamble, one thing's for sure: these folks can lay better odds on discovering great food here than they can on great fortune.

THE MEADOWS

Some 12 thousand years ago, a lush marsh thrived in what is now the Nevada desert. In 1829, a Mexican scouting party stumbled on an oasis fed by ancient springs, calling it Las Vegas, "the meadows." Though the Mormons were the first group to actually settle in the area (in 1855), it was the advent of the railroad that led to the founding of Las Vegas on May 15, 1905. Construction of the railroad and Hoover Dam turned Vegas into another kind of watering hole. In the 1930s, legalized gambling (without regulations) created fertile ground for organized crime and fostered the town's no-holds-barred reputation. Casinos sprang up downtown to accommodate the serious gamblers who were flooding into the area. In 1941, El Rancho resort opened on a lonely length of highway leading to downtown, triggering a spate of building on the stretch now known as "The Strip."

Glamour came too, in the form of the Flamingo Hotel, a ritzy "carpet joint" founded by mobster Benjamin "Bugsy" Siegel in 1946. Hard on the Flamingo's heels followed the Tropicana, the Stardust, and the Sands, where the famed Rat Pack performed. Sin City was in full swing. Feeding the early iniquity were prodigious quantities of chuck-wagon chow. In an effort to keep guests on the property throughout the night, El Rancho's owner

©Mark Gibson

laid out a "Midnight Chuck Wagon Buffet" (all you could eat for a dollar), birthing a popular dining concept that continues to this day—albeit with posh theme décor and freshly made offerings.

CORPORATE CAPITAL AND CELEBRITY CHEFS

In the late 1960s, legal reform allowed publicly traded corporations to obtain gambling licenses, adding to the Vegas boom. But 20 years later, when casino-style gambling arrived in Atlantic City, New Jersey, suddenly, Las Vegas had some competition. Indeed, everything seemed as if it had been on the buffet a little too long. Enter entrepreneur Steve Wynn, who changed the face of Vegas when he built the city's first mega-resort—the 3,044-room, $630-million Mirage—in 1989. Soon the old hotels were being imploded to make way for fantastic new properties where one could joust with King Arthur, dine in the Eiffel Tower, or take a gondola ride along Venice's Grand Canal.

Toque trumped toga when Wolfgang Puck came to Caesars Palace in 1992, and celebrity chefs have been hedging their bets in Vegas ever since. Especially with the arrival of two of France's most esteemed chefs, Guy Savoy and Joël Robuchon, the city is being heralded as a culinary destination—and a pricey one at that.

In keeping with the trend toward local, seasonal, and sustainably raised ingredients, Vegas chefs are partnering with area farmers as well as with the 1,000-acre farm at the University of Nevada in an effort to stock their kitchens with local produce. So while Sin City's past— culinary and otherwise— may be a little unsavory, Las Vegas is clearly raising the stakes for a full-flavored future.

History

11

Where to **eat**

Alphabetical list of restaurants

Where to **eat** ▶ Alphabetical list of restaurants

Restaurants by cuisine type

American

Bistro Zinc	✗	122
Country Club (The)	✗✗	45
David Burke	✗✗	50
Joe's	✗✗	65
Rosemary's	✗✗	161
STACK	✗✗	99
Table 10	✗✗	106
Table 34	✗	142
Top of the World	✗✗	109

Asian

China Grill	✗✗	43
Chinois	✗	44
Grand Wok & Sushi Bar	✗	60
Koi	✗✗	66
Marssa	✗✗	133
Noodles	✗	76
Noodle Shop (The)	✗	77
Social House	✗✗	97
Tao	✗✗	107
Zine	✗	116

Barbecue

Lucille's Smokehouse Barbeque	✗	131
Rub	✗	162

Brazilian

Pampas	✗✗	81

Californian

Nobhill	✗✗✗	75
Spago	✗✗	98

Caribbean

rumjungle	✗✗	91

Chinese

Empress Court	✗✗✗	55
Fin	✗✗	58
Pearl	✗✗✗	82
Ping Pang Pong	✗	160
Red 8	✗✗	88
Wing Lei ✿	✗✗✗✗	114

Contemporary

Alex ✿✿	✗✗✗✗✗	30
Aureole ✿	✗✗✗	33
Bradley Ogden ✿	✗✗✗	39
DJT ✿	✗✗✗✗	151
Fleur de Lys	✗✗✗	59
Joël Robuchon ✿✿✿	✗✗✗	64
Kilawat	✗✗✗	128
L'Atelier de Joël Robuchon ✿	✗✗	67
Medici Café	✗✗✗	134
Michael Mina ✿	✗✗✗	70
miX ✿	✗✗✗	71
Postrio	✗✗✗	85
Verandah	✗✗✗	113

French

Alizé ✿	✗✗✗	148
Andre's (Monte Carlo)	✗✗✗	31
Andre's (Downtown) ✿	✗✗	172
Bouchon	✗✗	38
Daniel Boulud Brasserie ✿	✗✗✗	49
Eiffel Tower	✗✗✗	53
Guy Savoy ✿✿	✗✗✗✗	61
Le Cirque ✿	✗✗✗	68
Marché Bacchus	✗	155
Mon Ami Gabi	✗✗	72
Morels	✗✗	74
Pinot Brasserie	✗✗	84

Fusion

SUSHISAMBA	✗✗	104
Todd's Unique Dining	✗	144

Gastropub

J.C. Wooloughan	✗	154

German

Hofbräuhaus	✗	126

Indian

Gandhi	✗	124
Gaylord India	✗✗	153
India Palace	✗	127
Origin India	✗✗	136

International

Sensi	✗✗	94

Italian

Ago	✗✗✗	120
Antonio's	✗✗✗	149
Bartolotta	✗✗✗	34
B & B Ristorante	✗✗	35
Dal Toro	✗	48
Enoteca San Marco	✗	56
Ferraro's	✗✗	152
Fiamma	✗✗	57
Grotto	✗	174
Il Mulino	✗✗	62
Marc's	✗✗	156
Nora's Cuisine	✗	158
Nove Italiano	✗✗	159
Osteria Del Circo	✗✗✗	80
Pasta Shop & Ristorante	✗	137
Piero's	✗✗✗	138
Rao's	✗✗	87
Stratta	✗✗	100
Terra Rossa	✗✗	165
Terra Verde	✗✗	143
Trattoria del Lupo	✗✗	110
Trevi	✗✗	111
Valentino	✗✗✗	112

Japanese

Nobu ✿	✗✗	135
Okada	✗✗✗	78
Sen of Japan	✗	163
Shibuya	✗✗	95
Shizen	✗	164
Sushi Roku	✗✗	103
SushiWa	✗	141
Yellowtail	✗✗	115

Mediterranean

Olives	✗✗	79
Picasso ✿✿	✗✗✗✗	83
Vintner Grill	✗✗	167

Mexican

Border Grill	✗✗	37
Casa Don Juan	✗	173
Diego	✗	52
Isla	✗✗	63
Lindo Michoacán	✗	129
Pink Taco	✗	139
Taqueria Cañonita	✗✗	108
Viva Mercado's	✗	168

Moroccan

Marrakech	✗	132

Pizza

Settebello	✗	140

Seafood

Aquaknox	✗✗✗	32
Emeril's	✗✗	54
Restaurant Charlie ✿	✗✗✗	89
rm seafood	✗✗✗	90
SeaBlue	✗✗	92

Southwestern

Mesa Grill	✗✗	69

Spanish

Firefly	✗	123

Steakhouse

A.J.'s Steakhouse	✗✗✗	121
BOA Steakhouse	✗✗	36
Capital Grille (The)	✗✗✗	40
Carnevino	✗✗	41
Charlie Palmer Steak	✗✗✗	42
Craftsteak	✗✗✗	46
CUT	✗✗✗	47
Hank's Fine Steaks & Martinis	✗✗✗	125
N9NE	✗✗✗	157
Prime Steakhouse	✗✗✗	86
Smith & Wollensky	✗✗✗	96
Strip House	✗✗	101
Stripsteak	✗✗	102
SW Steakhouse	✗✗✗	105
Vic & Anthony's	✗✗✗	175

Thai

Archi's Thai Kitchen	✗	150
Lotus of Siam	✗	130
Thai Spice	✗	166

Cuisine type by area

THE STRIP

American
Country Club (The)	✗✗	45
David Burke	✗✗	50
Joe's	✗✗	65
STACK	✗✗	99
Table 10	✗✗	106
Top of the World	✗✗	109

Asian
China Grill	✗✗	43
Chinois	✗	44
Grand Wok & Sushi Bar	✗	60
Koi	✗✗	66
Noodles	✗	76
Noodle Shop (The)	✗	77
Social House	✗✗	97
Tao	✗✗	107
Zine	✗	116

Brazilian
Pampas	✗✗	81

Californian
Nobhill	✗✗✗	75
Spago	✗✗	98

Caribbean
rumjungle	✗✗	91

Chinese
Empress Court	✗✗✗	55
Fin	✗✗	58
Pearl	✗✗✗	82
Red 8	✗✗	88
Wing Lei ✿	✗✗✗✗	114

Contemporary
Alex ✿✿✿	✗✗✗✗✗	30
Aureole ✿	✗✗✗	33
Bradley Ogden ✿	✗✗✗	39
Fleur de Lys ✿	✗✗✗	59
Joël Robuchon ✿✿✿	✗✗✗✗	64
L'Atelier de Joël Robuchon ✿	✗✗	67
Michael Mina ✿	✗✗✗	70
miX ✿	✗✗✗	71
Postrio	✗✗✗	85
Verandah	✗✗✗	113

French
Andre's (Monte Carlo)	✗✗✗	31
Bouchon	✗✗	38
Daniel Boulud Brasserie ✿	✗✗✗	49
Eiffel Tower	✗✗✗	53
Guy Savoy ✿✿	✗✗✗✗	61
Le Cirque ✿	✗✗✗	68
Mon Ami Gabi	✗✗	72
Morels	✗✗	74
Pinot Brasserie	✗✗	84

Fusion
SUSHISAMBA	✗✗	104

International
Sensi	✗✗	94

Italian
Bartolotta	✗✗✗	34
B & B Ristorante	✗✗	35
Dal Toro	✗	48
Enoteca San Marco	✗	56
Fiamma	✗✗	57
Il Mulino	✗✗	62
Osteria Del Circo	✗✗✗	80
Rao's	✗✗	87
Stratta	✗✗	100
Trattoria del Lupo	✗✗	110
Trevi	✗✗	111
Valentino	✗✗✗	112

Japanese
Okada	✗✗✗	78
Shibuya	✗✗	95
Sushi Roku	✗✗	103
Yellowtail	✗✗	115

Mediterranean
Olives	✗✗	79
Picasso ✿✿	✗✗✗✗	83

Mexican
Border Grill	✗✗	37
Diego	✗	52
Isla	✗✗	63
Taqueria Cañonita	✗✗	108

Seafood
Aquaknox	✗✗✗	32
Emeril's	✗✗	54
Restaurant Charlie ✿	✗✗✗	89
rm seafood	✗✗✗	90
SeaBlue	✗✗	92

Southwestern
Mesa Grill	✗✗	69

Steakhouse
BOA Steakhouse	✗✗	36
Capital Grille (The)	✗✗✗	40
Carnevino	✗✗	41
Charlie Palmer Steak	✗✗✗	42

Where to **eat** ▶ Cuisine type by area

Starred restaurants

*W*ithin the selection we offer you, some restaurants deserve to be highlighted for their particularly good cuisine. When giving one, two or three Michelin stars, there are a number of things that we judge, including the quality of the ingredients, the technical skill and flair that goes into their preparation, the blend and clarity of flavors, and the balance of the menu. Just as important is the ability to produce excellent cooking time and again. We make as many visits as we need, so that our readers can be sure of quality and consistency.

A two- or three-star restaurant has to offer something very special in its cuisine; a real element of creativity, originality or "personality" that sets it apart from the rest. Three stars —our highest award—are given to the very best restaurants, where the whole dining experience is superb.

Cuisine in any style, modern or traditional, may be eligible for a star. Because we apply the same independent standards everywhere, the awards have become benchmarks of reliability and excellence in more than 20 European countries, particularly in France, where we have awarded stars for almost 80 years, and where the expression "Now that's real three-star quality!" has entered into the language.

The awarding of a star is based solely on the quality of the cuisine.

Exceptional cuisine, worth a special journey.

One always eats here extremely well, sometimes superbly.
Distinctive dishes are precisely executed, using superlative
ingredients.

Joël Robuchon	𝕏𝕏𝕏𝕏	64

Excellent cuisine, worth a detour.

Skillfully and carefully crafted dishes of outsanding quality.

Alex	𝕏𝕏𝕏𝕏𝕏	30
Guy Savoy	𝕏𝕏𝕏𝕏	61
Picasso	𝕏𝕏𝕏𝕏	83

A very good restaurant in its category.

A place offering cuisine prepared to a consistently high standard.

Alizé	𝕏𝕏𝕏	148
Andre's (Downtown)	𝕏𝕏	172
Aureole	𝕏𝕏𝕏	33
Bradley Ogden	𝕏𝕏𝕏	39
Daniel Boulud Brasserie	𝕏𝕏𝕏	49
DJT	𝕏𝕏𝕏𝕏	151
L'Atelier de Joël Robuchon	𝕏𝕏	67
Le Cirque	𝕏𝕏𝕏	68
Michael Mina	𝕏𝕏𝕏	70
miX	𝕏𝕏𝕏	71
Nobu	𝕏𝕏	135
Restaurant Charlie	𝕏𝕏𝕏	89
Wing Lei	𝕏𝕏𝕏𝕏	114

Where to **eat** ▶ Starred restaurants

Buffets

In the days before Las Vegas became an oasis of fine dining, buffets were the favored dining choice at Las Vegas hotels, catering to crowds who subscribe to the philosophy that more is more insofar as food is concerned. If you're staying at a resort on or near The Strip, chances are your hotel offers a buffet. These all-you-can-eat abbondanzas typically feature enormous dining rooms and a wide array of cuisines arranged at different stations, where patrons serve themselves to as many helpings as their appetite will allow. Advertising a reasonable price tag, these groaning boards are normally open for breakfast, lunch and dinner. Lunch usually runs under $20 per person, and dinner rolls in at less than $30. Beverage service is included, with the exception of alcoholic beverages.

In recent years, buffets have traded rows of chafing dishes, heat lamps, and steam tables for impressive food displays, diverse ethnic options, and even dishes cooked to order in some cases. Items span the globe and run the gamut from fried chicken and prime rib to sushi, tacos, and crêpes. For those who find it difficult to tear themselves away from the casino to eat, the game of Keno is frequently available in many buffet dining rooms.

The following is a brief list of buffets that meets our standards of good quality and value.

Restaurants by hotel

Where to eat for less than $25

Archi's Thai Kitchen	✕	150
Casa Don Juan	✕	173
Firefly	✕	123
Gandhi	✕	124
Hofbräuhaus	✕	126
India Palace	✕	127
J.C. Wooloughan	✕	154
Noodles	✕	76
Nora's Cuisine	✕	158
Ping Pang Pong	✕	160
Settebello	✕	140
Thai Spice	✕	166
Viva Mercado's	✕	168

Where to have lunch

Archi's Thai Kitchen	✗	150		Noodles	✗	76
Bistro Zinc	✗	122		Noodle Shop (The)	✗	77
BOA Steakhouse	✗✗	36		Nora's Cuisine	✗	158
Border Grill	✗✗	37		Olives	✗✗	79
Capital Grille (The)	✗✗✗	40		Origin India	✗✗	136
Casa Don Juan	✗	173		Pampas	✗✗	81
Country Club (The)	✗✗	45		Ping Pang Pong	✗	160
Dal Toro	✗	48		Pink Taco	✗	139
David Burke	✗✗	50		Pinot Brasserie	✗✗	84
Eiffel Tower	✗✗✗	53		Postrio	✗✗✗	85
Emeril's	✗✗	54		Rao's	✗✗	87
Enoteca San Marco	✗	56		Red 8	✗✗	88
Ferraro's	✗✗	152		rm seafood	✗✗✗	90
Fin	✗✗	58		Rosemary's	✗✗	161
Firefly	✗	123		rumjungle	✗✗	91
Gandhi	✗	124		Sensi	✗✗	94
Gaylord India	✗✗	153		Settebello	✗	140
Grand Wok & Sushi Bar	✗	60		Smith & Wollensky	✗✗✗	96
Grotto	✗	174		Spago	✗✗	98
Hofbräuhaus	✗	126		Sushi Roku	✗✗	103
Il Mulino	✗✗	62		SUSHISAMBA	✗✗	104
India Palace	✗	127		SushiWa	✗	141
J.C. Wooloughan	✗	154		Table 10	✗✗	106
Joe's	✗✗	65		Table 34	✗	142
Kilawat	✗✗✗	128		Taqueria Cañonita	✗✗	108
Lindo Michoacan	✗	129		Terra Rossa	✗✗	165
Lotus of Siam	✗	130		Thai Spice	✗	166
Lucille's Smokehouse Barbeque	✗	131		Top of the World	✗✗	109
Marché Bacchus	✗	165		Trevi	✗✗	111
Marc's	✗✗	156		Valentino	✗✗✗	112
Medici Café	✗✗✗	134		Verandah	✗✗✗	113
Mesa Grill	✗✗	69		Vintner Grill	✗✗	167
Mon Ami Gabi	✗✗	72		Viva Mercado's	✗	168
Morels	✗✗	74		Zine	✗	116

Where to have a late dinner

THE STRIP

B & B Ristorante	✗✗	35
Bradley Ogden ✿	✗✗✗	39
Carnevino	✗✗	41
China Grill	✗✗	43
Dal Toro	✗	48
Enoteca San Marco	✗	56
Fin	✗✗	58
Mesa Grill	✗✗	69
Mon Ami Gabi	✗✗	72
Morels	✗✗	74
Noodles	✗	76
Noodle Shop (The)	✗	77
Red 8	✗✗	88
Smith & Wollensky	✗✗✗	96
Social House	✗✗	97
Stratta	✗✗	100
Strip House	✗✗	101
SUSHISAMBA	✗✗	104
Table 10	✗✗	106
Tao	✗✗	107
Taqueria Cañonita	✗✗	108
Trevi	✗✗	111
Valentino	✗✗✗	112
Yellowtail	✗✗	115
Zine	✗	116

EAST OF THE STRIP

Ago	✗✗✗	120
A.J.'s Steakhouse	✗✗✗	121
Firefly	✗	123
Lindo Michoacán	✗	129
Origin India	✗✗	136

WEST OF THE STRIP

Ferraro's	✗✗	152
Ping Pang Pong	✗	160
Sen of Japan	✗	163

DOWNTOWN

Vic & Anthony's	✗✗✗	175

Where to eat ▶ Where to have a late dinner

The Strip

To locate restaurants in selected Strip resorts, refer to floorplans in the Where to Stay section.

The Strip

A carnival of neon lights and eye-popping architecture, The Strip, boasting the city's largest collection of resorts and casinos, lies along a 4.5 mile stretch of Las Vegas Boulevard, beginning at Stratosphere running south to Mandalay Bay.

The Desert Blooms

When the first casinos sprang up downtown, The Strip was a vacant length of Highway 91 to the south. After Nevada legislation legalized gambling in 1931, El Rancho Vegas opened its doors; the location enabled the owner to avoid taxes and building restrictions within city limits. The 1941 hotel was followed by The Last Frontier and The Flamingo Hotel (famed as mobster Bugsy Siegel's "carpet joint"). By the early 1950s, the Las Vegas Strip—so dubbed by police officer and owner of The Last Frontier—came into its own as The Sands, Dunes, and Stardust raised their heads.

Eras of Extravagance

By the '60s, resorts along The Strip eclipsed downtown venues. 1989 introduced the

28

first mega-casino-resorts on Las Vegas Boulevard with Steve Wynn's Mirage—cities unto themselves with luxurious guestrooms, plush casinos, fine restaurants, spas, shopping arcades, theaters, lush pool environments, and just about anything you can imagine.

Then 1993 rang in an era of the imploding casino, bringing down The Dunes, Landmark, Sands, and Stardust with Vegas-worthy pomp, pyrotechnics, and cheering crowds.

For the past two decades, The Strip abounds with amazing hotels, profiles ranging from a 30-story pyramid and scale model of la Tour Eiffel to Steve Wynn's eponymous, soaring glass tower.

A monorail now connects properties east of Las Vegas Boulevard between The Sahara and MGM Grand. Entertainment has changed over the years too, from Rat Pack crooners to headliners like Barry Manilow, Bette Midler, and Elton John.

The Vegas skyline rises ever higher with new hotels—the Trump International Tower and The Palazzo (opened in 2008). A host of new residential/hotels are slated to pop up on The Strip later this year. City Center, a sleek multi-use urban complex replete with condos, casino hotels, and space for retail, dining, and entertainment is under construction and scheduled for completion by 2009.

© Mark Gibson

The Strip

Alex ✿ ✿ (Wynn)

B2 — Contemporary 𝕏𝕏𝕏𝕏𝕏

3131 Las Vegas Blvd. S.

Phone: 702-770-3300
Web: www.wynnlasvegas.com
Prices: **$$$$**

Thu – Mon dinner only

The walls of the lavishly appointed Alex have probably seen more proposals, anniversaries, and graduation celebrations than most of the other restaurants in Vegas, and for good reason. From its picture-perfect location in the Wynn hotel to its lush, ornate interior—replete with a gleaming marble staircase, polished wood, and dripping chandeliers—Alex cuts an impressive figure (for which you'll want a jacket).

Sit back and let the expert team tend to your every whim while indulging in the nightly tasting menu of Alessandro Stratta, who taps his Italian-French heritage for inspiration. Dinner might begin with a highly stylized Napoleon, comprised of fresh liquorice sheets, crunchy, briny caviar, and tiny cubes of deep red bluefin and pale konpachi; or end with six fluffy coins of blini, served over a complex, perfectly-poached rhubarb and a scoop of *vin santo* ice cream.

Appetizers
- Seared Diver Scallops with Sea Urchin, White Asparagus Gratin and Ponzu Sabayon
- Seared Hudson Valley Foie Gras with Orange-braised Fennel and Aromatic Spices

Entrées
- Japanese "Amadai" with Sweet Potato Tempura, Horseradish Cream and Red Wine Jus
- Wagyu Beef with Fava Bean Purée, Root-Crop Bean Salad and Bordelaise Sauce

Desserts
- Meyer Lemon Gratin with Vanilla Citrus
- Chocolate Cherry Port Caramel

Andre's (Monte Carlo)

French 🍴🍴🍴

3770 Las Vegas Blvd. S.

Phone: 702-798-7151   Dinner daily
Web: www.andrelv.com
Prices: $$$$

Middle and most elegant sibling in André Rochat's family of three Las Vegas restaurants, Andre's at the Monte Carlo succeeds in its aim to re-create the ambience of a Renaissance-era French château. From the recessed, hand-painted ceiling and the Versace chargers, to the crimson U-shaped booths that nuzzle intimate alcoves along the perimeter of the small room, the décor bespeaks a tranquility centuries removed from the modern world.

Classic, uncomplicated, and French at their core, the recipes here lean more toward the contemporary (think pan-roasted diver scallops with celery-root purée) than the menu at the original Andre's downtown. Courses wheeled to the table on carts, and plates covered by silver domes represent formal but not stuffy service, which pays special attention to detail.

A circular staircase winds upstairs to the two-story, glassed-in wine cellar.

Aquaknox (Venetian)

B3

Seafood 🍴🍴🍴

3355 Las Vegas Blvd. S.

Phone: 702-414-3772
Web: www.aquaknox.net
Prices: $$$

Dinner daily

Shimmering like the sea in cool deep blues and silver accents, Aquaknox shines its spotlight on "global water cuisine." The large lounge area in the entry greets guests with loud club music, and presents a dazzling raw bar piled high with mussels, oysters, prawns, clams, stone crab claws, and more. The main dining room sports a lively scene; while the calmer back room boasts a view of the open kitchen.

Chef Tom Moloney, a protégé of Wolfgang Puck, trolls the world's oceans for the freshest catch and flies them in daily. The likes of Maine scallops, Tai snapper, King salmon, and Ahi tuna find their way to this desert oasis. Grilled, sautéed, or seared, the seafood is enhanced with fragrant broths and piquant sauces.

Gracious and professional servers pluck wines from the cylindrical walk-in cellar, which is surrounded by a rushing water wall at the front of the restaurant.

Aureole  (Mandalay Bay)

Contemporary XXX

A-B5

3950 Las Vegas Blvd. S.

Phone: 702-632-7401 Dinner daily
Web: www.aureolelv.com
Prices: $$$$

Before you even descend the marble staircase that leads you into Aureole's sleek, contemporary dining room, you see it— a gleaming, beautiful 42-foot-high glass and stainless-steel wine tower. Inside the tower, a beautiful woman in a black cat suit and harness is climbing her way up and around over 10,000 wine bottles in the temperature-controlled space. That would be one of Charlie Palmer's famed "wine angels," inspired by the film *Mission Impossible*. Quite a show, even for Vegas—and the food has no trouble competing.

With two inspired nightly tasting menus that might include a silky tartare of ruby-red Ahi tuna with a delicate crispy spring roll as a centerpiece; tender quail, roasted to a pitch-perfect golden brown and filled with creamy foie gras stuffing; and a decadent tiramisu parfait, served in a glass tumbler with a luscious brownie as a sidekick.

Appetizers

- Trio of Ahi Tuna "Mediterranean"
- Chicken Terrine with Leeks and Summer Truffles
- Roasted Beets and Buffalo Mozzarella, with Pear-Balsamic Sorbet

Entrées

- Veal Sweetbreads and Herb-crusted Tenderloin, Morels, English Peas
- Roasted Monkfish with Saffron Risotto
- Duck Breast, Rhubarb Confit, Roasted Fennel, Crisp Polenta Cake

Desserts

- Black Mission Fig and Ricotta Cheesecake Tart
- Concord Grape Float with Warm Grape Tart and Sour Cream Ice Cream
- Chocolate-Hazelnut Crunch Cake with Hazelnut Bombe

Bartolotta (Wynn)

Italian 🍴🍴🍴

The Strip

B2

3131 Las Vegas Blvd. S.

Phone: 702-770-9966   Dinner daily
Web: www.wynnlasvegas.com
Prices: $$$$

Fishing for fine seafood in Las Vegas? You need cast your line no farther than the Esplanade at Wynn, where Bartolotta will fill the bill swimmingly. Follow the winding staircase down into the main dining room, an ocean of opulence awash in smooth marble and rich fabrics.

Paul Bartolotta, former chef and managing partner at Chicago's popular Spiagga, brings his love of Italian cuisine to his kitchen in the desert. Here, his heritage and affinity for wild-caught seafood results in a menu that flaunts whole fish flown in fresh daily from the waters surrounding Italy. Although it's pricey to order a whole fish ($14 and up for 3 ounces), you'll nonetheless net the likes of a perfectly baked, delicate Mediterranean snapper, served tableside with a flourish.

For the *ne plus ultra* in romance, request one of the tented cabana tables that circle the tranquil pool outside.

B & B Ristorante (Venetian)

Italian 🍴

B3

3355 Las Vegas Blvd. S.

Phone: 702-266-9977
Web: www.bandbristorante.com
Prices: $$$

Dinner daily

It was only a matter of time until celebrity chef, Mario Batali, added his culinary can-can—performed, of course, in his signature orange Crocs—to the Sin City restaurant lineup. His first Vegas venture, with partner and winemaker Joseph Bastianich, has been kicking up a fuss at the Venetian since it opened in spring 2007.

Rustic finesse marks the courses here, each prepared with care and products of excellent quality. The menu, which includes a handful of dishes from the chef's ever-popular Babbo in New York City, proffers an intriguing selection that roams the regions of Italy. From Tuscany, warm tripe "alla parmiagiana" sits in a spicy tomato sauce under a cap of melted Parmesan cheese. Barbecued squab lies on a bed of roasted beet "farrotto" and porcini mushrooms.

As an encore, Batali followed with casual Enoteca San Marco, located upstairs in the Grand Canal Shoppes.

BOA Steakhouse (Caesars Palace)

Steakhouse ✗✗

The Forum Shops, 3500 Las Vegas Blvd. S.
Phone: 702-733-7373
Web: www.innovativedining.com
Prices: $$$

Lunch & dinner daily

With two hip sisters in Los Angeles, this upscale steakhouse imports Hollywood panache to the top floor of the Forum Shops in Caesars Palace.

As far as prices go, the stakes are high here, though lunch is more affordable for those having a bad run at the tables (perfectly prepared sandwiches include a "fully loaded" burger, prime tenderloin, and seared Ahi tuna). At dinner, New York strip steak dry-aged for 40 days vies with premium Japanese Wagyu beef and Kobe flatiron for attention. All meat entrées come with your choice of rubs, crusts, and sauces. As the menu states, "any turf can surf" with lobster, King crab legs, or prawns; there is also a separate selection of seafood entrées.

The very "L.A." décor features padded ultrasuede walls, a towering glass-enclosed wine cellar, and ghostly trees of sandblasted driftwood that "grow" out of the center of the room.

Border Grill (Mandalay Bay)

Mexican ✗✗

3950 Las Vegas Blvd. S.

Phone: 702-632-7403
Web: www.bordergrill.com
Prices: $$

Lunch & dinner daily

Mary Sue Milliken and Susan Feniger located the Vegas outpost of their Santa Monica flagship halfway between the casino and the Convention Center at Mandalay Bay, where it is a prime lunch spot for convention attendees. The Sin City Border Grill maintains the upbeat Latin music, the casual atmosphere, and the tasty, well-prepared Mexican cuisine for which its older sister is known.

Two dining levels both include patios that gaze out over the resort's pool area. If you're ensconced in your lounge chair by the water, there's no need to move far—poolside patio dining offers the likes of grilled fish tacos, rock shrimp ceviche, and quesadillas filled with honey- and chipotle-marinated carne asada—not to mention icy, refreshing margaritas and mojitos.

Hotel guests can even dine in their bathing suits at The Cantina's laid-back take-out taqueria.

Bouchon (Venetian)

French 🍴

B3

3355 Las Vegas Blvd. S.

Phone: 702-414-6200
Web: www.venetian.com
Prices: $$

Mon – Fri dinner only
Sat – Sun lunch & dinner

Cousin of Thomas Keller's original Bouchon in the Napa Valley, the Venetian's rendition is similar in many respects. Both restaurants share the same menu, with one exception: the Vegas Bouchon is open for breakfast. This isn't your standard hotel breakfast, though; the menu here features quiche, *boudin blanc, croque madame,* and baked eggs Florentine—not to mention fresh-baked brioches and flaky chocolate croissants. Dinner adds standard bistro *plats principaux* from steak frites and *poulet rôti* (roasted chicken) to trout amandine and gnocchi *à la Parisienne.*

With its pewter bar, mosaic-tile floor, and hand-painted murals, Bouchon's setting in the Venezia Tower will make you long for lingering meals in Lyon—minus the palm trees, of course, which are unique to this desert locale.

If you're hoping to have lunch here, you'll have to come on a weekend.

Bradley Ogden ✿ (Caesars Palace)

Contemporary ✗✗✗

B3

3570 Las Vegas Blvd. S.

Phone: 702-731-7731   Dinner daily
Web: www.caesarspalace.com
Prices: $$$$

Now six years into its stay at Caesars' Palace, Chef Bradley Ogden's self-titled restaurant may be more subdued in style than most Vegas establishments (the earth-toned dining room could use a makeover), but the food still ignites the senses—with the California-minded kitchen spinning a modern, eco-friendly menu that draws from some of the better farms across the country.

Kick your meal off with four plump, pan-seared diver scallops, touched with lemongrass foam, and puddled in a creamy clam chowder; or two soft Jonah crab cakes, perfectly crusted on the outside and tender inside, with a lush side of eggplants and mushrooms in a black pepper sauce. Afterwards, linger over a moist little coconut rum cake, topped with fresh fruit and a smooth scoop of vanilla ice cream.

Sports fans will want to grab a seat at the bar, where you can enjoy ace food while catching the game.

Appetizers	*Entrées*	*Desserts*
• Maytag Blue Cheese Soufflé & South Dakota Bison, Pecan-stuffed Pear	• Pork Trio, Squash Spoon Bread, Apple-Celery Sauce	• Meyer Lemon & Huckleberry Pie, Elderflower Gelée
• Frog Legs, Parsley Root Espuma, Meyer Lemon Gremolata	• Pan-seared Char, Heirloom Beet Napoleon, Roasted Cauliflower	• Gingerbread-Toffee Pudding, Eggnog Ice Cream
• Organic Chestnut Soup, Fuji Apple Ravioli	• Roasted Chicken, Risotto, Grain Mustard Sauce	• Peppermint-Chocolate Cobbler

The Capital Grille

Steakhouse ✗✗✗

Fashion Show Mall, 3200 Las Vegas Blvd. S.
(at Spring Mountain Rd.)

Phone: 702-932-6631
Web: www.thecapitalgrille.com
Prices: $$$

Mon – Sat lunch & dinner
Sun dinner only

Find this comfortable, satisfying, and well-run steakhouse on the third level of Fashion Show Mall, across the street from Wynn Las Vegas. Also uncover locations of this well-known chain in other cities across the U.S., including New York, Chicago, and Dallas.

In this Sin City satellite, a well-dressed clientele comes for classic steakhouse fare, which spotlights beef dry-aged on the premises. From the porcini-rubbed Delmonico to the double-cut lamb rib chops, meat is the main attraction here. Broiled Atlantic lobster (sized from two to five pounds); seared citrus-glazed tuna; and grilled swordfish jardinière make waves on the seafood menu.

Split into several sections, the dining room overlooks the Strip from its second-floor glass-walled perch. Here, it promotes a pleasantly animated, clubby art deco atmosphere, enhanced by mahogany wood, copper accents, and low lighting.

The Capital Grille

Carnevino (Palazzo)

Steakhouse ✗✗

B2

3325 Las Vegas Blvd. S.

Phone: 702-789-4141 Dinner daily
Web: www.carnevino.com
Prices: $$$$

Two classic duos, Mario Batali and Joe Bastianich marry steak and wine at their new restaurant in The Palazzo. A large bronze bull stands at Carnevino's entrance—a portent of dishes to come.

Indeed, meat steers the menu, with all-natural house-aged beef starring in a filet mignon, seared crisp on the outside while remaining moist and tender inside. A vinaigrette tinged with bits of black truffle lends an earthy tang. Other options range from veal scaloppine to lamb chops "Scottadita"— a Batali signature. Though portions are generous, a meal here can add up fast; sauces and accompaniments are priced à la carte. Pastas, such as a rich, herb-infused potato gnocchi Bolognese, are available in half-portions in case you want to order one as a *primi*.

Formal Italian style and 16-foot ceilings decorate the two main dining areas, arranged on either side of a Palazzo hallway.

41

Charlie Palmer Steak (Mandalay Bay)

Steakhouse

 A-B5

Four Seasons, 3960 Las Vegas Blvd. S.

Phone: 702-632-5120   Dinner daily
Web: www.charliepalmer.com
Prices: $$$$

Leafy plants, varnished woods, and warm gold tones create a swanky restaurant, befitting Charlie Palmer's steakhouse setting, off the lobby of the posh Four Seasons Hotel (which occupies floors 35 to 39 of Mandalay Bay at the south end of the Strip).

On this pleasant changing menu of both classic and some modern fare, Japanese Wagyu beef may share the bill with a charcoal-grilled aged filet mignon; a 16-ounce thyme-basted veal Delmonico; a fire-roasted Sonoma chicken; and a stuffed Maine lobster. The long selection of side items ranges from Parmesan potato gratin and gruyère gnocchi to creamed sweet corn, and garlic *broccolini*.

The dining room can get noisy, thanks to the boisterous bar crowd separated from the spacious dining room only by a wood and glass partition; but the good news is that you won't have to traipse through a clanging casino to access this restaurant.

China Grill (Mandalay Bay)

Asian XX

3950 Las Vegas Blvd. S.

Dinner daily

Phone: 702-632-7404
Web: www.chinagrillmgt.com
Prices: $$$$

Located off the main casino floor, China Grill brings guests inside via a glass bridge that spans a trickling water feature. At the front of the restaurant, a sunken, dimly lit lounge caters to the cocktail crowd; while beyond, the multilevel dining room sports a futuristic look designed by Jeffrey Beers to incorporate a palette of rich dark colors and a domed planetarium-style ceiling illuminated with colored lights.

Flavorful dishes here express a wide variety of Asian influences. Large portions of ginger and garlic-spiked beef and scallion dumplings; Shanghai lobster; and sake-marinated "drunken" chicken are perfect for sharing among a group of business colleagues or friends.

China Grill is part of a group of restaurants (under the auspices of Jeffrey Chodorow's China Grill Management) that started in Manhattan and now extends as far away as Mexico City.

43

Chinois (Caesars Palace)

Asian ✗

The Forum Shops, 3500 Las Vegas Blvd. S.

Phone: 702-737-9700
Web: www.wolfgangpuck.com
Prices: $$

Fri – Sun lunch & dinner
Mon – Thu dinner only

East meets the Old West at Chinois. Located in the Forum Shops, Chinois is the little sister of the original Chinois on Main, which opened in Santa Monica in 1998. Like its sibling, the Vegas outpost honors the original concept with its modernized Hong Kong and Cantonese cuisine. The menu gallops from sushi to banana spring rolls; and from Sichuan noodles to Wolfgang Puck signatures: steamed fillet of Hong Kong salmon served with a citrus-soy sauce atop stir-fried vegetables; or the ever-popular Chinois chicken salad dressed in a sweet mustard-ginger vinaigrette. Dishes are done family-style, so corral a hungry crowd and chow down to your heart's content. Tea lovers will appreciate the excellent selection of premium blends.

Sleek and spacious, the bi-level main room incorporates Asian artifacts in its design, as well as an indoor terrace for people-watching.

Wolfgang Puck Fine Dining Group

The Country Club (Wynn)

American ✗✗

B2

3131 Las Vegas Blvd. S.

Phone: 702-770-3315

Lunch & dinner daily

Web: www.wynnlasvegas.com

Prices: $$$$

Open to golfers, golf enthusiasts, and non-golfers alike, Steve Wynn's interpretation of an upscale golf club boasts panoramic views of the lush rolling fairways and the 18th-hole waterfall on Wynn's golf course. Inside, plaid carpets, dark woods, white leather chairs, granite-topped tables, and vintage black-and-white photographs (of golfers, naturally) set a classy scene. On warm, sunny days, tables on the outdoor patio, which runs the length of the dining room, are par for the course.

The club bills itself as a "steakhouse," even though its menu drives way beyond traditional fare to include simple but flavorful, high-quality American dishes. Many relish a 20-ounce rib chop or a 16-ounce New York strip, but the likes of free-range chicken with corn-mushroom succotash, and Chilean sea bass with cauliflower purée are just as likely to hit a hole-in-one.

45

Craftsteak (MGM Grand)

Steakhouse

3799 Las Vegas Blvd. S.

Phone: 702-891-7318   Dinner daily
Web: www.mgmgrand.com
Prices: $$$$

The craft of cooking comes to the fore at Chef Tom Colicchio's contemporary steakhouse. Located on MGM Grand's Studio Walk, Craftsteak focuses on the purity of premium ingredients in its straightforward food. The unique mix-and-match concept allows diners to craft their own meal from a daily changing list of first courses, entrées, and side dishes. Perhaps you'll pair a grilled ribeye steak with roasted Maui onions and sweet potato purée; or match Nantucket Bay scallops with mushroom risotto and Italian kale … it's all up to you. Several three-course chef's menus assist the more indecisive diner, and the expansive wine list accommodates a wide range of budgets.

Attentive servers populate the dining room, decorated in organic earth tones and natural materials. Craftsteak's concept was so successful in Vegas that it spawned a sibling in New York City.

CUT (Palazzo)

B2

Steakhouse ☓☓☓

3325 Las Vegas Blvd. S.

Phone: 702-607-6300   Dinner daily
Web: www.wolfgangpuck.com
Prices: $$$$

A cut way above the standard Vegas steakhouse, Wolfgang Puck's new entry into the Sin City dining arena marks the entrance to the Shoppes at The Palazzo. This is the little sister to the original Cut, set inside the opulent Beverly Wilshire in Los Angeles. Modern and bold, the masculine design is a study in smoky gray offset by leather-covered tables and cube-shaped glass light fixtures.

An evening here kicks off with a tableside introduction to the different cuts of American and Japanese Wagyu beef. The former ranks as USDA Prime, corn-fed and dry-aged; the latter is the real thing from Kagoshima Prefecture. Global influences redefine the dishes, as in Kobe beef short ribs spiced Indian-style with coriander, ginger, cardamom, and star anise. Extra touches—warm cheese *gougères* as a prelude to the meal—attentive servers, and a well-clad clientele contribute to the pleasure.

Dal Toro (Palazzo)

Italian ✗

3325 Las Vegas Blvd. S.

Phone: 702-437-9800   Lunch & dinner daily
Web: www.palazzolasvegas.com
Prices: $$

File this one under "Only in Vegas." Even if you can't afford to take home a Lamborghini from the adjacent showroom, feel free to drool over them as you tuck into your linguini in the dealership's cafe. The restaurant's name echoes Lamborghini's iconic bull; and the ultra-modern design keeps pace with vibrant colors—a red Murano glass chandelier, and an outdoor patio surrounded by 100 feet of marbled mosaic Palladian-style fountains.

As for the rest, the chef is Italian, the food is authentic, and the portions are big enough to make you confident you're getting your money's worth—though, those who come to buy a car here are hardly concerned about price. Lasagna *della nonna* credits the chef's grandmother for its rich, tasty recipe: layers of homemade noodles layered with sausage, meat ragù, marinara, prosciutto *cotto*, hard-boiled egg, fresh mozzarella, and pecorino cheese.

Tom Donoghue

Daniel Boulud Brasserie ✿ (Wynn)

French 🍴🍴🍴

B2

3131 Las Vegas Blvd. S.

Phone: 702-248-3463
Web: www.wynnlasvegas.com
Prices: $$$

Dinner daily

Wynn Las Vegas

How the great Daniel Boulud does a Vegas brasserie—with an elegant, upscale dining room dressed in shades of pale, a romantic outdoor terrace overlooking the lake, and windows that dance with color from the Wynn hotel's hypnotic light-and-waterfall show. A beautiful design, undoubtedly, but if you're looking for that bawdy brasserie fix, turn to the menu—which offers a straightforward mix of the usual French suspects, rendered by Executive Chef Wes Holton.

Appetizers of super-fresh Maine lobster on a bed of avocado purée and fennel, or a soft, perfectly-seared salmon served with black trumpet mushrooms and squash, are right on the money.

Post feast, look to the excellent cheese and charcuterie collection to pair with a glass of wine; or a stunning dessert of soufflé Grand Marnier, made fresh to order with a cool citrus salad and scoop of creamy yogurt on the side.

Appetizers
- Torte of Duck, Guinea Hen, and Foie Gras
- Lobster Salad with Celery, Pickled Rhubarb, Pistachio
- Chilled English Pea Soup, Asparagus-Brie Quiche

Entrées
- Loup de Mer, Sauce Vierge, Artichoke, Olives
- Braised Short Ribs "En Daube", Ramps, Fava, Potato
- Kurobuta Pork, Gnocchi, Rapini, and Green Apple

Desserts
- Raspberry & Pistachio Tart, Lavender Honey
- Grand Marnier Soufflé, Citrus Salad, Yogurt Ice Cream
- Cocoa-crusted Profiteroles, Rocky Road Ice Cream

49

David Burke (Venetian)

American XX

3355 Las Vegas Blvd. S.

Phone: 702-414-7111
Web: www.davidburkelasvegas.net
Prices: $$$

Mon – Fri lunch & dinner
Sat – Sun dinner only

Named for its founder, New York City celebrity chef and entrepreneur, David Burke, this spacious, casual-chic dining room centers on a free-falling "waterfall" that rains down on a reed-like sculpture fashioned from red glass. It's a flashy—and often noisy—scene, with the sounds of the crowded room and the animated open kitchen echoing off the high ceilings.

On Burke's menu, bold takes on American cuisine culminate in courses such as a starter of day boat scallops Benedict, with chorizo standing in for the customary Canadian bacon; or a main course of fresh black cod, sautéed and served with a spinach jus, hon-shimeji mushrooms, and a shaving of black truffle. Typical of a town in which excess rules, the hearty portions here are not for the faint of appetite.

A generous selection (more than 50) of wines by the glass is included on the international wine list.

Sharing the nature of infinity

Route du Fort-de-Brégançon - 83250 La Londe-les-Maures - Tél. 33 (0)4 94 01 53 53
Fax 33 (0)4 94 01 53 54 - domaines-ott.com - ott.particuliers@domaines-ott.com

Diego (MGM Grand)

B4

Mexican 🍴

3799 Las Vegas Blvd. S.

Phone: 702-891-3200

Web: www.mgmgrand.com

Prices: $$$

Dinner daily

Round up some friends and make your way to this lively Mexican restaurant at the far end of Studio Walk. Casual and boisterous, done in hot colors (bright pink, tangerine, neon green) that are as loud as the salsa music, Diego promises tons of fun, south-of-the-border-style. The bar is a popular place to meet and greet; bet on the extensive list of tequilas to wash away any gaming woes.

Start with the house guacamole, prepared tableside; or the shrimp cocktail—citrus-poached rock shrimp, mixed in a cocktail shaker at your table with freshly squeezed lime juice and prickly-pear ice, before being poured into a martini glass layered with diced avocado, fresh salsa, fried corn kernels, and toasted pumpkin seeds. Then move on to copious portions of signature dishes like *carne asada à la Oaxaca* (ribeye steak bathed in flavorful mole); or *cochinita pibil* (braised pork).

Eiffel Tower (Paris)

French ✕✕✕

B3

3655 Las Vegas Blvd. S.

Phone: 702-948-6937
Web: www.eiffeltowerrestaurant.com
Prices: $$$$

Lunch & dinner daily

A romantic aura swirls around you as you step off the glass elevator on the 11th floor of the replica Eiffel Tower in Paris—the hotel. Every table has a stunning view in this dimly lit dining space, which juxtaposes cozy booths and plush red chairs with the girders that compose the tower. Below, through the floor-to-ceiling windows, glitters another city of lights—Las Vegas.

This restaurant is a place in which to celebrate. Conceived by Chef Jean Joho of Chicago's sky-high restaurant Everest, the menu of French cuisine here proves nearly as arresting as the breathtaking view. A multicourse prix-fixe option complements an à la carte selection that might feature lemon-poached Lake Superior white fish; a venison chop with wild huckleberries; and individual beef Wellingtons.

For dessert, one of the ethereal soufflés makes a fittingly lofty ending to a meal *chez la Tour Eiffel*.

Emeril's (MGM Grand)

Seafood

B4

3799 Las Vegas Blvd. S.

Phone: 702-891-7374
Web: www.mgmgrand.com
Prices: $$$

Lunch & dinner daily

Emeril Lagasse kicks up the MGM Grand with a bite of the Big Easy at his New Orleans-style fish house. At the entrance, a large metal fish sculpture gives the first clue to the theme here. The marine motif continues with glowing blue tones, wavelike wood accents, and curved booths upholstered to resemble fish scales. Tall, glassed-in wine-storage units provide pleasant focal points.

Spices and flavors combine in unique ways in such seafood creations as pecan-crusted Texas redfish with Creole meunière butter, and seared bacon-wrapped Gulf shrimp napped with sweet-corn poblano-chile cream. A Grand Cru espresso will finish your meal with a "bam!"

Can't get enough of Emeril? Check out the menu page that catalogs a collection of signature apparel and other *Emerilabilia* for sale.

Empress Court (Caesars Palace)

Chinese XXX

B3

3570 Las Vegas Blvd. S.

Phone: 702-731-7731
Web: www.caesarspalace.com
Prices: $$$

Wed – Sun dinner only

An oasis of serenity far from the clatter of the casino floor, Empress Court reveals itself as a grand columned rotunda as you step off the elevator; located next to Rao's (*see restaurant listing*), between two bronze Chinese lions. The room soars as a night-sky ceiling twinkling with stars. From these heights, fabric panels cascade down into the center of a room filled with well-spaced, round tables topped with bowls of orchids. From the terrace, view Caesar's palm-studded Garden of the Gods Pool.

Well-heeled connoisseurs of Hong Kong-style Cantonese haute cuisine may begin their meal with a crafted cocktail such as Blue Sapphire or a Lychee martini. Then they must choose between an expanse of categories including noodles, abalone, beef, fresh seafood, tofu, and vegetables.

Fit for royalty, two multicourse tastings—The Emperor and The Empress—showcase the chef's talent to best advantage.

Enoteca San Marco (Venetian)

B3

Italian ✗

Grand Canal Shoppes, 3377 Las Vegas Blvd. S.

Phone: 702-677-3390

Lunch & dinner daily

Web: www.enotecasanmarco.com

Prices: $$

For a casual Italian meal and a front-row seat for the circus of entertainment taking place in the Piazza San Marco, make tracks for this *enoteca*, brought to Vegas by the team of Mario Batali and Joe Bastianich.

Carne (sliced cured meats), *fritti* (fried appetizers), salads, and vegetables introduce the all-day menu—the first two are particularly tasty. Pasta, pizza, and *piatti* (perhaps crispy duck; swordfish Livornese; and veal and ricotta meatballs) fill in as main courses. Large portions mean that sharing is the best way to try options from each category. Finish with the selection of cheeses or desserts, along with a cup of expertly made espresso or cappuccino.

Come late afternoon, a seat at one of the closely spaced tables or at the marble counter—ideal for solo diners and parties of two—makes a great spot to savor a quartino of wine and some *salumi* to tide you over until dinner.

Fiamma (MGM Grand)

Italian ✕✕

B4

3799 Las Vegas Blvd. S.

Phone: 702-891-7600
Web: www.mgmgrand.com
Prices: $$$

Dinner daily

Fans of SoHo's Fiamma Osteria can now enjoy the similarly well-prepared Italian food and well-selected wine list in the desert. Stylish and casual, this Fiamma can be found on MGM Studio Walk, next to the theater where the Cirque de Soleil show KÀ plays, making it a good spot for a pre-performance meal.

Wood forms the core of the organic design, from the twisting wood slats that screen diners from passers-by to the woven wood panels that divide the room into sections. In the lounge, an open fireplace and a sculptural "wave wall" suggesting desert dunes lend a sensuous quality.

Spaghetti and meatballs reaches new heights here with fresh-cut *chitarra* pasta, Kobe meatballs, and San Marzano tomatoes. Dishes such as "Piemontese" braised beef short ribs and whole grilled branzino will ignite your taste buds—an experience befitting a restaurant whose name means "flame" in Italian.

Fin (Mirage)

Chinese ✕✕

B3

3400 Las Vegas Blvd. S.

Phone: 702-791-7111
Web: www.mirage.com
Prices: $$

Thu – Mon lunch & dinner

Strings of smoky glass "pearls" hang like curtains at Fin, dividing the serene space into intimate smaller sections. Backlit illustrated panels along the walls diffuse the light in a room colored by chocolate-brown wood and accented by dark gray and ecru.

Despite this lovely restaurant's location right off the clanging casino floor, the service here is on the formal side—smooth, discreet, and knowledgeable. When you're tired of guessing your odds at the casino, count on Fin to double down on a large array of Chinese cuisine, most of it familiar. A hot pot of braised and fried tofu with black mushrooms and vegetables; Kung Pao chicken or shrimp; Cantonese barbecued duck; chow mein; and a large selection of live seafood are just a sampling of the range of cooking styles, spices, textures, and ingredients that are seriously interpreted here.

MGM Mirage

Fleur de Lys (Mandalay Bay)

Contemporary ✗✗✗

A-B5

3950 Las Vegas Blvd. S.

Phone: 702-632-9400
Web: www.mandalaybay.com
Prices: $$$$

Dinner daily

Follow the walkway leading toward Mandalay Bay's convention center to find the Vegas branch of Chef Hubert Keller's famed San Francisco restaurant. Sophisticated yet relaxed, the organic space introduces drama with its 30-foot-high, sand-colored stone walls and 12,000-bottle wine loft. Focal point of the dining room, a striking leaf-shaped frame filled with thousands of fresh rose blossoms adorns one wall.

For dinner, the Alsatian-born chef has designed three, four, and five-course prix-fixe menu options. Each menu is based on an appetizer, entrée, and dessert, with options to add a fish course and a cheese course. French regionals lie at the heart of the wine list, which remembers America with a good selection of California and Oregon labels.

Flickering candlelight casts an intimate glow on the closely spaced tables, and several cabanas along the wall create private retreats.

Grand Wok & Sushi Bar (MGM Grand)

B4

Asian ✗

3799 Las Vegas Blvd. S.

Phone: 800-929-1111
Web: www.mgmgrand.com
Prices: $$

Lunch & dinner daily

Slightly elevated off the MGM Grand casino floor, the Grand Wok's entrance is designated by blond wood, black granite accents and a bubbling water feature. Inside the sleek space, thick glass panels shield the dining room from the cacophony of the slot machines while offering views of all the action.

Taking its cues from China, Japan, Thailand, Korea, Vietnam, and Malaysia, the cuisine at Grand Wok features Asian dishes from spicy Kung Pao chicken and seafood clay pot to sushi rolls and fragrant Thai noodle soup. Fresh ingredients yield flavorful food, served in portions large enough to satisfy the most robust appetites.

One caveat: the Grand Wok is open for lunch and dinner; but on weekdays if it's sushi or sashimi you crave, you'll have to wait until dinnertime since the sushi bar is only open in the evening.

Guy Savoy ✿✿ (Caesars Palace)

French 🍴🍴🍴🍴

B3

3570 Las Vegas Blvd. S.

Phone: 702-731-7286
Web: www.guysavoy.com
Prices: $$$$

Wed – Sun dinner only

How celebrated French chef Guy Savoy does the Strip—with a gorgeous, minimalist design courtesy of Jean-Michel Wilmotte; an exacting and gracious service staff; and a nightly tasting menu that will transport you straight to France.

In Caesars' Augustus Tower, this beautiful restaurant is a confident little sister to its Parisian sibling. With a 1,000-deep wine list, a jackets-required policy, and a menu that boasts, among other delights, Savoy's famed artichoke and black truffle soup, salty-sharp with shavings of aged parmesan and served with a flaky toasted brioche warm with truffle butter for dunking.

Save room for a coconut dessert rendered six ways, each more mouth-watering than the next. From dried coconut chips to icy coconut granité to coconut meat prepared in a Southeast Asian style—each delicious bite is a study in contrasting textures, influences, and techniques.

Appetizers
- Artichoke and Black Truffle Soup
- Mosaic of Milk-fed Poularde, Foie Gras, and Celery Root with Black Truffle Jus
- Oysters in Ice Gelée

Entrées
- Maine Lobster, Carrots, Orange, and Star Anise
- Foie Gras-stuffed Rabbit Saddle, Mushrooms, Confit, Turnips
- Roasted Veal Chop, Braised Vegetables

Desserts
- Grapefruit Terrine, Earl Grey Tea Sauce
- Chocolate Fondant, Crunchy Praline, and Chicory Cream
- Dessert Trolley: Ice Creams, Sorbets, and French Pastries

Il Mulino (Caesars Palace)

Italian ✗✗

B3

The Forum Shops, 3500 Las Vegas Blvd. S.

Phone: 702-492-6000
Web: www.ilmulino.com
Prices: $$$$

Mon – Sat lunch & dinner
Sun dinner only

Located on the top level of the labyrinthine Forum Shops, Il Mulino continues the tradition started more than 20 years ago by brothers Fernando and Gino Masci in Greenwich Village. Wrought-iron chandeliers; a claret-colored carpet; glass-front cabinets filled with wine bottles; and a display of mouth-watering products against one wall creates a cozy atmosphere.

Imported cheeses, olive oils, and salamis complement a menu that highlights the bold flavors of the Abruzzi region, home to the brothers Masci. A mix of visitors and locals frequent this place for heaping portions of slow-cooked, old-world specialties such as the pappardelle *di giourno*, veal Saltimbocca, and ricotta cheesecake. Prices are high, but everything is made to order and special requests are not a problem.

Il Mulino's corner perch accommodates a wall of windows and an open-air terrace that overlooks the Strip.

Isla (Treasure Island)

Mexican ✗✗

B2

3300 Las Vegas Blvd. S.

Phone: 702-894-7349
Web: www.treasureisland.com
Prices: $$

Dinner daily

Park your pirate ship outside and swagger on in to Isla. With lively Latin music, young, friendly servers, and a menu created by Mexican-born chef Richard Sandoval (of Pampano and Maya in New York City), Isla whips up good food and fun at Treasure Island. Enter through the tequila bar, where premium tequila is the quaff of choice—mixed into margaritas or enjoyed in a Goddess Elixir, prepared tableside by Isla's own sensual Tequila Goddess.

Don't get hung up at the bar, though, or you'll miss the main attraction: traditional Mexican dishes with a sexy modern twist. Several different types of guacamole are prepared tableside; grilled filet mignon comes with a cheese enchilada in mole sauce; and the chile relleno is presented in a luscious tomato broth with beef picadillo and Oaxaca cheese served alongside (instead of being stuffed into) the chile.

63

Joël Robuchon ✿✿✿ (MGM Grand)

B4

Contemporary XXXX

3799 Las Vegas Blvd. S.

Phone: 702-891-7925

Web: www.mgmgrand.com

Prices: $$$$

Dinner daily

Forget dinner and a show. Dinner at Joël Robuchon is the show—and you better don your jacket for this one. Prepare to be dazzled when you enter the famed French chef's eponymous restaurant. The striking interior—modeled after a 1930s French salon, has enough rich jewel tones, velvety banquettes, and dripping chandeliers to make you forget there's a clanking casino nearby.

A parade of culinary genius so lovingly crafted it wows the senses. There are two tasting menus presented nightly—and even the simpler one will set you back a few hundred—but the reward arrives with dishes like soft, warm gorgonzola custard, made fresh to order served with pear, tomato coulis, and sage; or fresh sea bass, topped with an airy dollop of lemongrass foam, served over tender baby leeks; or braised lamb shoulder, dancing in fragrant spices and served with black truffle couscous.

Appetizers

- Osetra Caviar, Gelée, and Cauliflower Cream
- Black Truffle in Pastry with Onions, and Smoked Ham
- Crispy Soft-boiled Egg, Smoked Salmon, Osetra Caviar

Entrées

- French Hen with Roasted Foie Gras, Braised Potatoes
- Sautéed Veal Chop, Herb Jus, Vegetable Mille-Feuille
- Sea Bass, Lemongrass Foam, Stewed Baby Leeks

Desserts

- Pink Grapefruit with Violets, Lychee Sorbet
- Warm Soufflé Perfumed with Yuzu and Banana Ice Cream
- Crunchy Pearls of Manjari, Mint Ice Cream

Joe's (Caesars Palace)

American ✗✗

B3

The Forum Shops, 3500 Las Vegas Blvd. S.

Phone: 702-792-9222
Web: www.icon.com/joes
Prices: $$

Lunch & dinner daily

Renowned for their stone-crab claws, Joe's has been a Miami icon since 1913, when Joe Weiss set up a little lunch counter on Miami Beach. In 2004, Joe's opened on the ground floor of the Forum Shops, to the delight of seafood lovers marooned in the desert.

Of all of the restaurant's dining spaces (the casual bar and the clubby main room), the indoor terrace facing the fountain and statuary in the airy atrium makes the grandest spot in which to savor fresh fish and shellfish (Madagascar shrimp, Dover sole, Florida grouper) flown in from around the world. Meat options include calf's liver, lamb chops, and bone-in signature steaks; but you haven't truly experienced Joe's until you try the stone crabs, hand-harvested from the Gulf of Mexico and served chilled with the creamy house mustard sauce.

A children's menu and carryout items are also available.

Joe's Seafood, Prime Steak and Stone Crab

Koi (Planet Hollywood)

B3

Asian ✖✖

3667 Las Vegas Blvd. S.

Phone: 702-454-4555

Dinner daily

Web: www.koirestaurant.com

Prices: $$$$

Stylish, hip, and trendy, Koi perfectly matches the vibe of the new Planet Hollywood hotel. The Vegas satellite is part of a family of restaurants that stretches from New York City to Bangkok.

Be sure to dress to impress at this see-and-be-seen scene, set on the hotel's second level above the casino floor. Curving lines flow through the swanky space, which includes a bar and lounge near the entrance, and a long sushi bar backed by smoked mirrors and shelves displaying white coral, orchids, and chunks of quartz. A lovely enclosed patio looks out on Bellagio's lake and its dazzling fountain shows.

In the cavernous main dining room, cold dishes might include crispy rice topped with spicy minced tuna; while hot signatures run to grilled tiger prawns paired with pearl onions, purple sweet potatoes, and a kumquat glaze. Service is friendly and efficient.

L'Atelier de Joël Robuchon ✿
(MGM Grand)

Contemporary ✗✗

B4

3799 Las Vegas Blvd. S.

Dinner daily

Phone: 702-891-7358
Web: www.mgmgrand.com
Prices: **$$$$**

Who would guess that the MGM Grand harbored not one, but two, elegant gems within its massive walls? Located on the hotel's casino floor, just next door to fancier sibling, Joël Robuchon, L'Atelier is styled after the celebrated chefs Parisian original, with a gorgeous, intimate studio vibe.

Join the stylish crowd at the polished granite bar, where you can watch the chef's work their magic in the open kitchen, and sink your teeth into any number of creative dishes and small plates—like a thick prosciutto, aged 18 months, and served with a salty crostini piled high with peppered tomato *concassé*; or silky, shelled mussels perfectly poached in curry and dancing in curry foam; or crispy, skin-on Guinea hen, cooked on the rotisserie and served in a warm fan of slices, with a lobe of seared foie gras and a creamy scoop of Robuchon's famed pommes purée.

Appetizers

- Crispy Langoustine Fritter with Basil Pesto
- Poached Baby Kussi Oysters with French Butter
- Mediterranean Vegetables Layered with Buffalo Mozzarella

Entrées

- Foie Gras-stuffed Free-range Quail with Truffled Mashed Potatoes
- Steak Tartare with Old-fashioned French Fries
- Lightly-seared Tuna Belly with Crispy Onion Rings

Desserts

- Raspberry Surprise within White Chocolate Sphere, Yuzu Ice Cream
- Green Chartreuse Soufflé, Pistachio Ice Cream
- "Chocolate Sensation"

Le Cirque ✿ (Bellagio)

B3

French ✗✗✗

3600 Las Vegas Blvd. S.

Phone: 702-693-8100
Web: www.bellagio.com
Prices: **$$$$**

Dinner daily

You'll need to don a jacket for this circus, but it's worth the trouble. Sirio Maccioni brings his legendary New York restaurant, Le Cirque, to the Strip's tony Bellagio hotel. Reprising the whimsical, but sophisticated, circus motif that lent its Manhattan cousin its theatrical flair, the Adam Tihany-designed interior boasts a dramatic silk rainbow canopied ceiling, and colorful old circus murals grace the walls.

In the kitchen, Chef David Werly spins a classically French menu, with a nightly tasting menu that might kick off with two crispy, smoky patties of tender chopped pig's feet, porcini mushrooms, and artichoke hearts, laced with a tangy Dijon vinaigrette; and move on to a fresh, flaky fillet of salmon, pan-roasted with cracked Sichuan peppercorns and freshly ground cardamom, served over savory coins of zucchini, squash, and cucumber.

Appetizers

- Roasted Sweetbreads, Morels, Asparagus, Pearl Onions, and "Bowtie" Arugula
- Roasted Scallops, Langoustine "En Kadaïf", Mosaic of Beets, Balsamic Dressing

Entrées

- Sea Bass, Crispy Potatoes, Braised Leeks, Wine Reduction
- Milk-fed Veal Chop, Brussels Sprouts Mousseline
- Pepper & Cardamom Roasted Salmon

Desserts

- Praline Mousse, White Chocolate Ice Cream, Hazelnut-Caramel Crunch, Chocolate Sauce
- Raspberry Milk Shake, Light Mascarpone Crème, Crunch of Feuilletine

Mesa Grill (Caesars Palace)

Southwestern ⚔️

B3

3570 Las Vegas Blvd. S.

Phone: 702-731-7731
Web: www.mesagrill.com
Prices: $$$

Lunch & dinner daily

Celebrity chef, Bobby Flay, shakes things up in Vegas at the western outpost of Mesa Grill, where bold flavors, primary colors, and a casino just adjacent mix it up in a recipe for success. The Caesars Palace location of Flay's popular New York City grill separates itself from the gaming tables by walls of tinted glass, leaving the focus on the display kitchen and the sophisticated dishes.

Zesty tastes of the southwest benefit from a lively Mexican flair here in a duo of spicy salmon and tuna tartare, served with red and green chile sauces, garnished with crispy slices of plantain and blue-corn flatbread. Pan-roasted Alaskan halibut gets a kick from a bright base of smoky red chile-tomato sauce, as pleasing to the eyes as it is to the palate.

Tequila is the quaff of choice here, and the bar pours a wide range of premium-quality tequila and mezcal offerings.

Michael Mina ❀ (Bellagio)

ontemporary 🍴🍴🍴

B3**

3600 Las Vegas Blvd. S.

Phone: 702-693-8199
Web: www.bellagio.com
Prices: $$$$

Dinner daily

The Strip**

There isn't an ocean for hours outside of Vegas, but you'll never know it when you place your bets on Michael Mina. San Francisco's seafood auteur has brought his award-winning recipes east—and, as usual, he's done so with style.

Wind your way through the Bellagio's stunning lobby, past the flower-studded Conservatory, until you find the lovely, wood-paneled dining room. From there, allow Mina's polished, pleasant staff to spoil you with the likes of smooth and creamy parsnip bisque, chock-a-block with tender, shredded Dungeness crab, and studded with buttered brioche croutons; a savory black mussel soufflé with a heavenly saffron-chardonnay cream poured tableside; or a thick medallion of Ahi tuna topped with Hudson Valley foie gras.

Don't forget to save room for one of Mina's signature trios, like creamy panna cotta rendered with coconut, mango, and passion fruit.

Appetizers
- Butter-poached Maine Lobster, Sweet Corn Crêpe, Thai Coconut Cream
- Tartare of Ahi Tuna, Sesame Oil, Toasted Pine Nuts, Garlic, Chiffonade of Mint

Entrées
- American "Kobe" Ribeye, with Potato Purée, Horseradish, Cabbage, Spinach, Bacon, Sour Cream, and Onion
- Maine Lobster Pot Pie: Baby Carrots, Fingerling Potatoes, Black Truffles

Desserts
- "Root Beer Float": Sassafras Ice Cream, Root Beer Sorbet, Chocolate Chip-Pecan Cookies
- Chocolate-Milk Chocolate Ice Cream, Sicilian Pistachio, Chai

miX (Mandalay Bay)

Contemporary XXX

A-B5

THEhotel, 3950 Las Vegas Blvd. S.

Phone: 702-632-9500
Web: www.chinagrillmgt.com
Prices: **$$$$**

Dinner daily

Those lucky enough to make their way to miX, located on the 64th floor of the Mandalay Bay hotel, aren't likely to want for a view. Grab a seat facing the windows, and you'll be treated to an aerial shot of the Strip and Greater Las Vegas. And that's nothing compared to the view facing the restaurant's interior. Alain Ducasse's Vegas darling is home to a stunning Patrick Jouin design, dressed in iridescent shades of pearl, gorgeous hand-blown glass, and sleek, curving staircases.

Of course, the real Ducasse magic happens on your plate—with tender pillows of gnocchi, tossed in a creamy mix of young asparagus spears, shaved Parmesan, and earthy morel mushrooms; or a whole roasted lobster, fresh from Maine and pulled from its shell, then piled onto the plate in sweet, bite-sized lumps of tender meat with a creamy curry, and a scoop of floral basmati rice.

Appetizers
- Tender Potato Gnocchi, Asparagus, Wild Mushrooms, Parmigiano
- Shrimp Cocktail with Spicy Tomato Syrup
- Bluefin Tuna Tartare, Crisp Vegetables, Satay Condiment

Entrées
- Roasted Maine Lobster "au Curry", Coconut Basmati Rice
- Bison Tenderloin, "Sauce au Poivre", Mixed Vegetables
- Roasted Duck Breast, Black Mission Figs, Turnips

Desserts
- miX "Candy Bar"
- Strawberry Composition: Panna Cotta Foam and Meringue
- Caramel Napoleon and Pear Sorbet

The Strip

Mon Ami Gabi (Paris)

French 🍴

B3

3655 Las Vegas Blvd. S.

Phone: 702-944-4224
Web: www.parislasvegas.com
Prices: $$

Lunch & dinner daily

Granted, Las Vegas Boulevard is no match for the Champs Elysée, but this is as close as you'll get to that ambience in Sin City. One of the few restaurants that offers an open-air terrace on the Strip, Mon Ami Gabi makes people-watching de rigueur (complete with misters to cool patrons during the sweltering dessert summers). The patio, nestled in the shadow of the Eiffel Tower at Paris Las Vegas, is an ever-popular dining spot. This French demoiselle flaunts its view of the Bellagio fountain show, which takes place right across the street.

Inside, professional service and Belle Epoque style abounds in the authentically re-created brasserie named for owner and chef, Gabino Sotelino. The menu mixes Gallic classics (roast chicken grand-mère; Dover sole meunière) with selections like shrimp cocktail, burgers, and a New York strip steak—a clear nod to American tastes.

Paris Las Vegas

Tierce Majeure

Morels (Palazzo)

French ✗✗

3325 Las Vegas Blvd. S.

Phone: 702-607-6333
Web: www.palazzolasvegas.com
Prices: $$$

Lunch & dinner daily

Opened in early 2008 at the new Palazzo hotel, Morels hits the jackpot with its updated twist on the traditional French brasserie. In terms of décor, that means chandeliers glittering with iridescent Italian glass "bubbles," and Art Deco-style portraits instead of vintage French posters.

A wonderful selection of artisan-made cheeses, both domestic and imported, sets this French steakhouse apart. Meanwhile, tableside preparations for two—the petite romaine heart salad, the 32-ounce *côte de bœuf*, and the rack of Colorado lamb—show off the kitchen's interactive style, and the comprehensive wine list splits its orientation between France and California. But it's the 30-day, dry-aged, prime Midwestern steak that stands out here. Keep your eyes on the fries—in this case, a side of pommes frites with house-made truffle mayonnaise—and you've got a sure winner.

Nobhill (MGM Grand)

Californian 🍴🍴🍴

B4

3799 Las Vegas Blvd. S.

Dinner dinner

Phone: 702-891-7337
Web: www.michaelmina.net
Prices: $$$$

Named for a ritzy and historic section of San Francisco, Nobhill embodies Michael Mina's idea of an urban neighborhood restaurant. In this case, though, the neighborhood is the Strip, and the décor downplays Vegas glitz for a sleek, sophisticated look. Swathed in tones of taupe and chocolate brown, the room encompasses booths that all bear the name of a different street in San Francisco, the city where Mina first established his renowned culinary reputation.

If you're dining with a group, the starters for the table—like the charcuterie board or the hors-d'œuvre sampler—make for some tasty sharing. Main courses stretch from crispy skin Japanese snapper to Colorado rack of lamb. Bread is baked fresh in the restaurant's steam oven and presented to each table on a heated slab of granite.

The waitstaff adheres to the three P's of service: polite, professional, and polished.

Noodles (Bellagio)

The Strip

3600 Las Vegas Blvd. S.
Phone: 702-693-7111
Web: www.bellagio.com
Prices:

Lunch & dinner daily

You'll find this little Asian eatery hidden behind a bank of slot machines next to the Salon Privé and the Baccarat room. No secret anymore, Noodles is well worth seeking out for its inexpensive Far East fare, which employs top-quality products.

Marble floors and a backlit display of apothecary jars filled with different types of—you guessed it—noodles highlight the décor, while the menu takes inspiration from different parts of Asia. Signatures such as roasted soya chicken (made with "ancient" soy sauce); vermicelli with pork knuckle; and premier fried rice with pineapple, sausage, pork floss, raisins, and shrimp number among the long list of tasty dishes. Sure bets are the spicy noodle soups, or the wok-fried noodle entrées.

Those looking for small bites will want to go for dim sum, served Friday to Sunday from 11am to 3pm.

The Noodle Shop (Mandalay Bay)

Asian ✕

A-B5

3950 Las Vegas Blvd. S.

Phone: 702-632-7800

Web: www.mandalaybay.com

Prices: $$

Lunch & dinner daily

Looking for a place to lunch in Mandalay Bay? Oodles of noodles are what you'll find at The Noodle Shop. Bold flavors and choice ingredients composing the Asian cuisine here will please your palate, while copious portions of dishes like chicken pad Thai, noodle soups, Cantonese beef stew, and Thousand Year egg and shredded pork congee will fill you up so you can spend more uninterrupted hours at the casino.

The recently renovated Asian cafe sports a sleek, contemporary design that stands in sharp contrast to its traditional menu. Speedy, friendly service and proximity to the hotel's convention center make this place a good bet for a casual midday meal in between business meetings—especially since it's one of the few restaurants in Mandalay Bay that is open for lunch. Perhaps best of all, it won't cost all your winnings to eat here.

Okada (Wynn)

Japanese XXX

B2

3131 Las Vegas Blvd. S.

Phone: 702-248-3463
Web: www.wynnlasvegas.com
Prices: $$$

Dinner daily

A popular—and rightly so—option for skillfully prepared Japanese cuisine in Las Vegas, Okada takes its title from a friend of Steve Wynn's who also happens to be an investor in the resort.

Chef Masa Ishizawa's food wanders the world of Japanese cuisine from sushi and sashimi to *robatayaki*. Lady Luck is shining on you if the menu specials include lobster miso soup, swimming with chunks of succulent lobster meat. One of the most-ordered items, Okada's rendition of a spicy tuna cut roll deliciously blends fresh minced tuna with red chili paste, scallions, and sesame oil.

Guests can dine at the sushi bar or at the semi-circular *robata* bar; revelers favor the sake bar for pre-dinner libations. Pendulous moon-like Japanese lanterns, a floating pagoda table, and a web of gigantic black chopsticks lining the ceiling compose a contemporary landscape that honors Japan's rich history.

Wynn Las Vegas

Olives (Bellagio)

Mediterranean ✗✗

B3

3600 Las Vegas Blvd. S.

Phone: 702-693-8255
Web: www.bellagio.com
Prices: $$$

Lunch & dinner daily

This is yet another outpost of Boston area celebrity, Chef Todd English, who has opened a number of restaurants with this particular concept across the country.

His contemporary Mediterranean fusion menu racks up points with signatures such as tuna carpaccio; fig and prosciutto flatbread; and, of course, the Olives burger, topped with balsamic-glazed onions and cheddar cheese. Here you'll find shareable portions of fun, flavorful food, all well thought out as to the way in which the ingredients complement each other.

While the Vegas varietal may not be the best performer in the Olives' orchard, it is nevertheless an enjoyable place for dinner. Low key at lunch, Olives comes alive in the evening when the main room and bar fill up with an animated crowd. The smart décor warms up then too, the dark woods and rich colors aglow under low light.

MGM Mirage

Osteria Del Circo (Bellagio)

Italian 🍴🍴🍴

B3

3600 Las Vegas Blvd. S.

Phone: 702-693-8150   Dinner daily
Web: www.osteriadelcirco.com
Prices: $$$$

Standing shoulder to shoulder with older sibling Le Cirque, this lighthearted osteria dazzles with blazing burgundy and gold hues and a big-top theme conceived by Adam Tihany. Refined Tuscan fare reigns supreme in this whimsical setting. In an attempt to tantalize your taste buds, the menu proposes a balanced array of clay-oven-baked pizzas, house-made pastas (the sheep's-milk ricotta ravioli in sage butter sauce comes highly recommended), fish, and meat dishes.

On the wine list, you'll discover some fine Barolos and Barbarescos schmoozing with an A-list of California labels. Service is sophisticated and surprisingly formal, so if you're looking for a casual atmosphere, camp out at the lively bar.

Pampas (Planet Hollywood)

Brazilian ✗✗

B3

Miracle Mile Shops, 3663 Las Vegas Blvd. S.

Phone: 702-737-4748
Web: www.pampasusa.com
Prices: $$

Lunch & dinner daily

The Strip

Calling all carnivores! Rope a bunch of buddies with big appetites and swagger on over to Pampas Churrascaria (in the Miracle Mile Shops) for a style of eating that originated centuries ago on the high plains of Southern Brazil. While you won't be sitting around a campfire under the stars, you will be treated to a robust repast of spit-roasted meat. Skewers of chicken, sirloin, pork loin, lamb, and more are carved to order at your table. Turn the disk on the table green-side-up to signal you want more. Had enough? Flip the disk to red. Think of it as an epicurean rendition of the children's game Red Light, Green Light.

Potent South American cocktails will get the party started. To follow, complimentary cheese bread, and fried banana and chickpea fritters are plenty tasty, but if you've simply got to have some veggies, head for the salad bar.

81

Pearl (MGM Grand)

Chinese XXX

B4

3799 Las Vegas Blvd. S.

Phone: 702-891-7380
Web: www.mgmgrand.com
Prices: $$$$

Dinner daily

Obscured by a panel of frosted glass, Pearl is discreetly cached away from the main casino floor along MGM Grand's Studio Walk. Well-dressed couples and business diners favor this elegant restaurant, outfitted by New York designer Tony Chi with bold red lamps, dark wood furnishings and teal enamel accent tiles. High-backed cream suede booths along the wall provide the most intimate seating option.

Upscale Chinese cuisine here spotlights premium ingredients, with a focus on live seafood. Dishes from the changing seasonal menu (think crispy salt and pepper squid, steamed live garlic shrimp, fire-roasted Mongolian beef) are plated with artistic flair and presented with a formal flourish.

A pot of fresh-brewed tea is the traditional way to end a meal at this gem of a restaurant; once on the table, the teapot keeps warm over a votive oil lamp.

Picasso ✿✿ (Bellagio)

Mediterranean 🗡🗡🗡🗡

B3

3600 Las Vegas Blvd. S.

Phone: 702-693-7223

Web: www.bellagio.com

Prices: $$$$

Wed – Mon dinner only

In a town filled with cheap, flashy numbers, it's time someone classed things up. Let's start with a jacket, which you'll need for Picasso. Next, let's get some real art in you. How about a wall filled with stunning original paintings by the master himself? If that doesn't do it, there's plenty more genius to be found on the plate—and the man behind those creations is the Spanish-born chef, Julian Serrano, who has manned the kitchen here since its inception. The exquisite fare includes a sweet boudin of fresh lobster, shrimp, and scallops, dancing with sun dried tomatoes and tomato coulis, and offset by a single, delicious roasted shrimp; or a fresh veal chop, perfectly roasted bone-in and flanked by a lovely gathering of vegetables cooked *sous vide*.

Grape hounds won't be disappointed by the wine list, which catalogues a healthy list of price ranges from across the globe.

Appetizers

- Butternut Squash Soup with Amaretto-Nutmeg Marshmallows
- Ragout of Vegetables, Foie Gras, Jus de Poularde
- Salpicon of Seared Tuna with Piquillo Pepper Oil

Entrées

- Roasted Milk-fed Veal Chop with Confit of Rosemary Potatoes
- Sautéed Medallions of Fallow Deer with Caramelized Apples and Zinfandel Sauce

Desserts

- Strawberry Napoleon, Vanilla Flan, Strawberry Vin de Glacé Jelly
- Rhubarb, Elderberry Jus with Lychee & Black Raspberry Swirl Sorbet
- Gianduja Mousse Gâteau, Nutella Gelato

83

Pinot Brasserie (Venetian)

French ✗✗

B3

3355 Las Vegas Blvd. S.

Phone: 702-414-8888

Web: www.patinagroup.com

Prices: $$$

Lunch & dinner daily

A member of Chef Joachim Splichal's Patina Restaurant Group, Pinot Brasserie adds a soupçon of French savoir faire to la dolce vita of The Venetian. The high-ceilinged space is decked out à la mode with antiques imported from France, red leather banquettes, and honey-toned wood paneling.

Open for breakfast, lunch, and dinner, the casual French cuisine will start your day off right with quiche Lorraine or eggs Florentine. At midday, come by for a *salade Niçoise* or a *croque Monsieur*. Dinnertime brings hearty main courses such as braised lamb shanks, seared sea scallops, and a 20-ounce Chateaubriand for two. And what would a French meal be *sans* dessert—as in a Tahitian vanilla crème brûlée or a bittersweet chocolate soufflé?

If you've got to dine and dash, you can grab a quick bite at the bar or get an espresso and a morning pastry to go at the bakery counter.

The Strip

Postrio (Venetian)

B3

Contemporary ✗✗✗

3355 Las Vegas Blvd. S.

Phone: 702-796-1110
Web: www.wolfgangpuck.com
Prices: $$$

Lunch & dinner daily

Wolfgang Puck's casual cafe borders the re-creation of St. Mark's Square in the Grand Canal Shoppes, where it makes the perfect respite from power shopping. Seemingly all that's missing from the original square in Venice are the pigeons, which you won't find on the terrace here. Seated under the artificial sky, you will enjoy a sunny, climate-controlled ambience all year round, no matter the weather outside.

The cafe is open for both lunch and dinner, but if it's a more sophisticated atmosphere you seek, you'll have to wait for evening to sup in the more formal interior dining room with its rich jewel tones and blown-glass chandeliers. Like big sister, Postrio in San Francisco, this Vegas sibling plays up changing entrées that have a global flair. Wood-oven-baked pizzas join pastas and small plates on the lunch menu, while dinner weighs in with a more elaborate selection.

Wolfgang Puck Fine Dining Group

85

Prime Steakhouse (Bellagio)

Steakhouse ✗✗✗

3600 Las Vegas Blvd. S.

Phone: 702-693-7111   Dinner daily
Web: www.bellagio.com
Prices: $$$$

The Strip

You expect high glamour from a chophouse on the Las Vegas Strip, but even so, Jean-Georges Vongerichten's lakeside version in Bellagio surprises with its lavish décor. Inspired by a 1930s-era speakeasy, Prime dons pale blue marble for its floor, sumptuous blue velvet to frame the opening to its rooms, and Baccarat crystal to add sparkle to its chandelier. Table settings are equally well outfitted, complete with soft lighting suited to romance. Amidst all this luxury, well-dressed is the way to go.

Top-quality meat dresses to impress in the likes of prime filet mignon, double-cut lamb chops and live Maine lobster. California's finest cabernets, merlots, and pinot noirs strut their stuff on the wine list, along with an excellent selection of French Bordeaux.

For an after-dinner drink or a cigar, the outdoor terrace facing the dancing fountains can't be beat.

Rao's (Caesars Palace)

Italian ✕✕

B3

3570 Las Vegas Blvd. S.

Phone: 877-346-4642
Web: www.raos.com
Prices: $$$

Lunch & dinner daily

Founded in East Harlem in 1896 by a family of Italian immigrants, this neighborhood red-sauce joint caught the attention of New York's culinary cognoscenti in 1977 when the *New York Times* gave it a rave review. Even now, it's nearly impossible to snag one of the restaurant's 11 tables, many of which are "reserved" for longstanding patrons.

Fortunately, you won't have that problem at Rao's in Caesars Palace, which replicates the Harlem original while accommodating nearly 300. Divided into smaller areas, the large dining room manages to feel intimate. An indoor/outdoor terrace, overlooking the hotel's Roman-style swimming pools, adds more seating.

As for the food, portions are generous and the flavor and quality of the products do not disappoint. Bet on generously sized plates of fresh-made fettucine alla Bolognese, and osso buco with saffron risotto to beat the house.

©Barry Johnson/ Harrah's

Red 8 (Wynn)

Chinese ✗✗

3131 Las Vegas Blvd. S.
Phone: 702-248-3463
Web: www.wynnlasvegas.com
Prices: $$

Lunch & dinner daily

In so many ways, Steve Wynn's classy signature hotel is over the top. That goes for many of its restaurants too. You won't have to hit it big at the roulette wheel to eat in Red 8, although this might just be your lucky number if you're looking to win at Wynn with reasonably priced Chinese fare.

Designed in high Asian style with red- and black-lacquer furnishings and a black and white mosaic tile floor, this restaurant lays out a broad menu of Southeast Asian favorites such as sweet and sour pork; steamed Chilean seabass; chili crab; and roast duck. If you're feeling adventurous, take a gamble on more unique items like shredded jellyfish marinated in sesame oil, or a bowl of noodles stocked with braised pork knuckle and fermented bean curd.

For partyers and nightowls, Red Eight offers late-night dining on weekends (Friday and Saturday until 1:00 A.M.). Dim sum is served for lunch on the weekends.

The Strip

Restaurant Charlie ✿ (Palazzo)

Seafood 🍴🍴🍴

B2

3325 Las Vegas Blvd. S.

Phone: 702-607-6336
Web: www.charlietrotters.com
Prices: $$$$

Dinner daily

It may have an everyman's moniker, but the luxurious cuisine of famed Chicago chef, Charlie Trotter, is anything but plain. Wind your way through the new Palazzo Resort, and just off the main casino floor you'll find a doorway leading to Bar Charlie—a stylish little lounge with a counter where you can indulge in a nightly kaiseki menu (Japanese-inspired haute cuisine). Behind it, you'll find the handsome new space that is Restaurant Charlie, with backlit geometric detailing and cozy, intimate banquettes flanked by polished wood.

The menu is dominated by Trotter's outstanding seafood creations, like tender rings of cuttlefish and Asian pear, dancing in a light sesame dressing studded with minced chervil; a fresh, flaky fillet of striped bass, sided with creamy saffron risotto; or tender hamachi, layered with braised veal cheek, and a handful of earthy morel mushrooms.

Appetizers
- Crab Salad with Sake and Rice Milk
- Salad of Asparagus, Rhubarb, Fennel, Nasturtium Leaves
- Braised Octopus, Olives, Serrano Ham and Peppers

Entrées
- Hamachi, Braised Veal Cheek and Morel Mushrooms
- Seared Sea Bream, Lemon, Chile, Cilantro
- Lamb Rack, Manchego Cheese and Cumin

Desserts
- Rhubarb Tapioca Pearl, Lychee, Green Tea Daifuku
- Fuji Apple Pie, Cheddar Cheese, Vanilla Ice Cream
- Sauternes-infused Pear, Muscovado Brioche, Queen of Jasmine Ice

rm seafood (Mandalay Bay)

Seafood

A-B5

Mandalay Place, 3930 Las Vegas Blvd. S.

Phone: 702-632-9300
Web: www.rmseafood.com
Prices: $$$$

Lunch & dinner daily

You'll find sleek rm seafood at the entrance to Mandalay Bay Place shopping area, upstairs from its casual sibling, Rbar cafe. You can't quibble with the caliber of the seafood here—it's first-rate.

Pristinely fresh (and caught or farmed in environmentally friendly ways) selections such as Hawaiian swordfish, branzino, or Maya prawns can be served grilled, broiled, sautéed, or blackened—your choice. There's a raw bar and a sushi menu too. The waitstaff doesn't always perform swimmingly, however; service tends to be out of sync with the quality of the food.

Along both walls of the upstairs room, banquettes cosset couples, while stand-alone tables accommodate larger groups in the center of the intimate dining room. Downstairs, Rbar dishes up bowls of clam chowder, platters of shellfish, and more in a laid-back atmosphere animated by three large plasma-screen TVs.

rumjungle (Mandalay Bay)

Caribbean ✕✕

3950 Las Vegas Blvd. S.

Phone: 702-632-7408

Web: www.chinagrillmgt.com

Prices: $$$

Lunch & dinner daily

A 22-foot-tall wall inset with rows of flickering flames beckons guests to rumjungle. Once inside, you'll be immersed in a club-like atmosphere in the three-tiered dining room. Jeffrey Beers' splashy décor feeds the senses with its zebra-striped tables, waterfalls, and gigantic conga drums that rise from the floor each evening as the restaurant morphs into a pulsating nightspot. A stylish crowd hovers around the circular bar, which is lit from underneath with a fluorescent green glow.

Dinner is the time to experience this place. Caribbean and Latin touches pepper dishes such as jerk-spiced chicken with Jamaican red beans and rice; dill mojo-marinated Altantic salmon; and a selection of meat and seafood cooked in the *rodizio* fire pit. The latter come with a choice of sides— perhaps caramelized ripe plantains or Cuban black beans and pineapple-coconut rice.

SeaBlue (MGM Grand)

Seafood

B4

3799 Las Vegas Blvd. S.

Phone: 702-891-3486
Web: www.michaelmina.net
Prices: $$$$

Dinner daily

Exuding the feeling of a contemporary brasserie, Michael Mina has a winner in this seafood-centric restaurant set along the Studio Walk. Here, interior designer Adam Tihany has outfitted SeaBlue's tony space with polished redbrick floors, vibrant red lantern-like light fixtures, and streaming water walls.

The menu doesn't flounder in its main ingredient: seafood that's flown in fresh daily. Well-developed flavors mark dishes (such as a tagine of North Sea cod; seafood paella; and a Kobe beef flatiron steak accompanied by olive oil smashed potatoes, broccoli rapini, and mushrooms) that dive deep into the cuisine of the Mediterranean and North Africa for their inspiration.

Check out the chefs as they create your meal in the open kitchen and at the two food-preparation areas located on one side of the three-sided bar in the middle of the room.

RAMOS PINTO

Est. 1880

Sensi (Bellagio)

International ✕✕

B3

3600 Las Vegas Blvd. S.

Phone: 702-693-8800
Web: www.bellagio.com
Prices: $$$

Lunch & dinner daily

Past Bellagio's lobby on the Via Fiore promenade, sensual Sensi decks itself out in modern and minimalist style with unpolished pink and gray granite, glass block, mirrored chrome, and rushing water walls.

The glass-enclosed kitchen, wild flames dancing on the stovetops, provides a focal point for diners. Here, Chef Martin Heierling crafts his 21st-century version of four different types of cuisine: Italian, Asian, seafood, and grilled dishes. Although the ingredients in this culinary voyage may be familiar, each mouthful provides clear, crisp palate teasers—from the sharp pucker of citrus and shallot in the tuna tartare quenelle to the distinct sweetness and herbaceous notes that caramelized vegetables and olives lend to the caponata.

Keeping pace with this world tour, the wine list spans the globe but its strength stays Down Under (the chef hails from New Zealand).

Shibuya (MGM Grand)

Japanese XX

B4

3799 Las Vegas Blvd. S.

Phone: 702-891-3001   Dinner daily
Web: www.mgmgrand.com
Prices: $$$$

From the room partitions fashioned of thin ribbons of wood to the backlit "canvas" of cube-shaped glass pieces that hangs above the sushi bar, Shibuya is as sleek and trendy as the Tokyo district for which the restaurant is named.

The long marble sushi bar at the front is a popular spot for solo diners. Here, sushi lovers will relish such fare as the Mifune roll, a flavorful combination of pieces of deep-fried softshell crab, crunchy batons of daikon and cucumber, fresh beads of tobiko, and julienne of carrot. It's all rolled up in nori and drizzled with a zesty red-chili aïoli. Beyond sushi, *teppanyaki* tables offer a wide selection of meat and seafood entrées as well as combinations of multiple elements.

Trust the waiters to make sound recommendations on the menu, and be sure to ask the knowledgeable sake sommelier for help navigating the extensive sake list.

Smith & Wollensky

B4

Steakhouse 🍴🍴🍴

3767 Las Vegas Blvd. S. (bet. Harmon & Tropicana Aves.)

Phone: 702-862-4100   Lunch & dinner daily
Web: www.smithandwollensky.com
Prices: $$$$

There's nothing small about this 635-seat steakhouse, brought to Vegas in 1998 as part of the well-known nationwide chain founded in Midtown Manhattan. USDA prime steaks (dry-aged and butchered in-house) weigh in at up to 18 ounces, and come with equally hefty price tags. As a starter, the shellfish "bouquet" overflows with lobster, oysters, shrimp, mussels, clams, and "colossal" lump crabmeat. Sides, from French fries to truffled macaroni and cheese, are sized for two—no exceptions.

Freestanding in a green and white building across from the Monte Carlo, Smith & Wollensky opens its Grill for lunch and late-night dining seven days a week, and even offers sidewalk seats on the Strip. Those foolhardy enough to brave the perpetual evening gridlock on Las Vegas Boulevard can take advantage of the restaurant's valet parking (offered at dinner only).

The Smith & Wollensky Restaurant Group

Social House (Treasure Island)

Asian ✗✗

3300 Las Vegas Blvd. S.

Phone:	702-894-7777	Dinner daily
Web:	www.socialhouselv.com
Prices:	$$

Come graze with the glitterati at TI's highly popular "it" restaurant. Take the elevator or climb the stairway lined with metal safe-deposit-like boxes to reach this oh-so-hip second-floor haunt. With its striking organic design by the New York firm AvroKo, Social House is the brainchild of the Pure Management Group (whose establishments include Pure and LAX).

The place is a bit schizophrenic, as if it can't decide between being a nightclub or a restaurant. And so it does both; DJs spin tunes each evening, and dining tables morph into conveyances for cocktails with the help of a hydraulic system. As expensive as it is expansive, the menu rolls out sushi and sashimi along with the likes of Kobe beef three ways, tamarind short ribs, and citrus peel miso-marinated cod.

Snag a seat on the outdoor patio for a front-row seat for the provocative Sirens of TI® show.

Spago (Caesars Palace)

Californian ✗✗

B3

The Forum Shops, 3500 Las Vegas Blvd. S.

Phone: 702-369-6300   Lunch & dinner daily
Web: www.wolfgangpuck.com
Prices: $$$

As is the case with many of the restaurants in Sin City's megaresorts, getting to Spago is a trek. You'll find the place in the Forum Shops, around the corner from the Fountain of the Gods. Along the way, you'll have to tear yourself away from the temptations posed by myriad pricey designer boutiques before you reach this casual cafe featuring "outdoor" seating in the mall.

This Wolfgang Puck concept began in Beverly Hills. At the Vegas branch, the cafe menu is as relaxed as the ambience, offering a selection of pastas, sandwiches, and salads—not to mention Puck's irresistible signature pizzas. Inside, the sleek and airy dining room (open for dinner only) kicks the décor and the cuisine options up a notch. Global influences are evident in such presentations as *choucroute garnie royale* (a traditional Alsatian dish), Kobe flatiron "Hunan style," and seafood paella.

STACK (Mirage)

American ╳╳

B3

3400 Las Vegas Blvd. S.

Phone: 702-791-7111   Dinner daily
Web: www.mirage.com
Prices: $$$$

In 2006, the Mirage stacked the odds in its favor by polishing up its fading image with the opening of Love™, the Cirque de Soleil show set to The Beatle's music. And, of course, what's a little image-enhancing without a couple of trendy restaurants?

STACK is one of these newer additions. Layered with undulating wood strips suggesting the walls of Nevada's nearby Red Rock Canyon, the restaurant envelops diners under its dark ceiling amid flickering candlelight. In the front of the room, the cool curving bar is the place to people-watch while you sip on house libations like the S'mores STACK martini, made with Stoli Vanil, chocolate Godiva, and Starbucks coffee liqueur.

Ponder the menu before you decide on American fare like the shellfish STACK, mini Kobe chili-cheese dogs, or the bone-in Brooklyn filet with an "XL" twice-baked potato on the side.

The Light Group

Stratta (Wynn)

B2

3131 Las Vegas Blvd. S.

Phone: 702-770-2040   Dinner daily
Web: www.wynnlasvegas.com
Prices: $$

In summer 2008, Chef Alex Stratta took over the reins at the restaurant formerly known as Corsa Cucina. He now lends his last name to this convivial cafe, while saving his first name for the more formal restaurant Alex, which he also oversees at Wynn.

Casual ambience complements straightforward and reasonably priced Italian cuisine here, which ranges from light (wood-fired *pizzette*) to hearty (veal parmigiana). Delicate flavors of chiles, olives, and mint balance a piece of roasted halibut, while osso bucco is a classic Milanese affair served with saffron risotto.

On the perimeter of Wynn's casino floor, the front dining room is done with white leather demilune benches flanking oval tables. In the more formal back section, bright red chairs, candlelight, and fabric panels dress up the area alongside the semi-open kitchen. Either space offers a good respite from gaming.

Strip House (Planet Hollywood)

Steakhouse ❌❌

B3

3667 Las Vegas Blvd. S.

Phone: 702-737-5200   Dinner daily
Web: www.striphouse.com
Prices: $$$$

With a saucy moniker like Strip House and a location like Vegas, your imagination could go wild here. Despite the setting on the Las Vegas Strip and the sensual black-and-white images of women that adorn the walls, the name of this restaurant refers to steak. The newest link in a chain by The Glazier Group, Strip House has satellites across the U.S.

A fantasy in deep red (textured red wallpaper and red leather banquettes) by David Rockwell forms a flashy backdrop for the likes of a manly New York strip (available in 16- or 20-ounce portions)—charred over high heat to sear in the flavor; or a tender rack of Colorado lamb. Desserts, such as the two-tiered cheesecake and the 24-layer chocolate cake, are enough to share around the table.

There's a lively scene at the bar, while the dining room offers a more subdued ambience. Three additional small rooms accommodate private parties.

Stripsteak (Mandalay Bay)

 A-B5

3950 Las Vegas Blvd. S.

Phone: 702-632-7414   Dinner daily
Web: www.michaelmina.net
Prices: $$$$

Known for his culinary talent with fish, Chef Michael Mina swims upstream from the Mandalay Bay's beach theme at Stripsteak, diving instead into all-natural, certified Angus beef. This boldly designed, modern steakhouse—one of the best in Las Vegas—appeals to manly appetites with slow-roasted prime rib, and steaks cooked to order on the wood-burning grill.

Innovative appetizers kick off a meal here with the likes of duck foie gras sliders and bite-size tuna sashimi "poppers" served with a refreshing ponzu sauce for dipping. Meat portions range from a 6-ounce Japanese "A5" Kobe filet mignon to a gut-busting 30-ounce Porterhouse.

Assuming you still have room for dessert (this will surely not be the case if you manage to finish the Porterhouse!), the Macallan 18-year butterscotch pudding accompanied by warm beignets will end your meal in style.

Sushi Roku (Caesars Palace)

Japanese ✗✗

B3

The Forum Shops, 3500 Las Vegas Blvd. S.

Phone: 702-733-7373

Web: www.sushiroku.com

Prices: $$

Lunch & dinner daily

Originally from Los Angeles, this gourmet sushi chain takes up residence on the third floor of the Forum Shops, where it seems right at home amid the Roman statues, stately fountains, and pricey boutiques. Inside, dark woods, bamboo, chiseled stone, and cascading water create a Zen vibe that is both cozy and hip.

In L.A. Sushi Roku is wildly acclaimed by the weight-conscious set; in Vegas this elegant place appeals for its range of Japanese fare, from tuna tataki salad with garlic ponzu to a Jidori chicken breast with homemade teriyaki sauce. Outstanding freshness and quality are evident in every bite of the sushi and sashimi (tuna belly, abalone, Japanese snapper, jumbo clam). High rollers may decide to go for the multicourse chef's omakase.

Sake is the drink of choice here, and the long list includes a sampler option with a tasting of three different grades.

Jeffrey Green

SUSHISAMBA (Palazzo)

Fusion 🍴🍴

B2

The Shoppes, 3327 Las Vegas Blvd. S.

Phone: 702-607-0700
Web: www.sushisamba.com
Prices: $$$

Lunch & dinner daily

Rounding out its restaurant lineup, the Palazzo introduces the Vegas outpost of the SUSHISAMBA chain. The same fusion of Brazilian, Peruvian, and Japanese cooking means that the menu runs from green bean tempura to Peruvian quinoa with barley and manchego cheese. You taste the delicious melding of cultures in a flaky rock fish à la plancha, seasoned with smoked chilis and served over grilled asparagus, segments of pink grapefruit, and zesty *tosa-su* sauce.

Located on the upper level of The Shoppes at The Palazzo, SUSHISAMBA draws the young and sexy set with its pumping music, stylish SUGARCANE lounge, and an exuberant décor that fills the tiered, 14,000-square-foot space with soaring ceilings, an elevated sushi bar, and colorful ribbons of swirling sculptural wood. Video screens throughout this hot spot project images of Rio's Carnival to encourage the festive party vibe.

The Palazzo

SW Steakhouse (Wynn)

Steakhouse ✗✗✗

B2

3131 Las Vegas Blvd. S.

Phone: 702-770-3325   Dinner daily
Web: www.wynnlasvegas.com
Prices: $$$$

From its early days as a gambling destination, Las Vegas has been a steakhouse town. That still holds true, though the quality of this genre has greatly improved over the years. SW Steakhouse proves the point as one of the best steakhouses in the city.

Ambience, service, and cuisine combine here to create a memorable dining experience. Descend the spiral escalator from the casino level under a canopy of colorful parasols and see for yourself. Sleek and polished, the dining room affords dramatic views of the Lake of Dreams, whose streaming water wall provides a serene backdrop on the lovely outdoor terrace.

The kitchen's execution hits its mark in a juicy grilled prime ribeye, charred on the outside and tender within. A trio of expertly made sauces perfectly complements the meat, and a list of add-ons ups the ante from crumbles of smoked blue cheese to roasted Sonoma foie gras.

Table 10 (Palazzo)

B2

American ✗✗

The Shoppes, 3327 Las Vegas Blvd. S.

Phone: 702-607-6363
Web: www.emerils.com
Prices: $$$

Lunch & dinner daily

As one of the hottest new properties on the Strip, the Palazzo has tapped some top chefs to splash their names across the hotel's restaurants. So, it's hardly surprising that Emeril Lagasse agreed to add his moniker to the mix. His new Vegas venture is named for an iconic table at Emeril's in New Orleans, where the chef would sit to design his menu, devise the wine list, and mentor his staff.

Reportedly the only kitchen in Las Vegas lit by natural light, Table 10 spins its menu compass around the country. Pasta jambalaya points south; lobster pot pie (with Nova Scotia lobster) points northeast; and Sonoma chicken from the restaurant's massive rotisserie points due west. Satisfying desserts, such as creamy sweet potato cheesecake and a new twist on a banana split, will end your meal in high-calorie style.

You can even purchase Emeril-branded food products and cookbooks here.

Tao (Venetian)

Asian ✕✕

B3

3355 Las Vegas Blvd. S.

Phone: 702-388-8338   Dinner daily
Web: www.taolasvegas.com
Prices: $$$

A sexy restaurant, nightclub, and lounge all under one roof, Tao splashed onto the Vegas scene in 2005. Sensual aptly describes the décor of the 42,000-square-foot, multilevel establishment, where gray stone water-filled vessels afloat with rose petals and flickering candles line the entrance; a two-story-tall statue of Buddha appears to float above a shimmering pool in the main dining room; a collection of hand-carved opium pipes fills one accent wall; and the hostesses are clad in sleek Chinese silk dresses.

Fresh premium Asian ingredients combine to form dishes that range from sushi and dim sum to shabu shabu, noodles, and roasted meats. Roasted Thai Buddha chicken, Hong Kong XO shrimp with long beans, and lo mein with roast pork will give you a hint of the menu. Go to eat, stay to party; the third level rocks at night as one of the hottest clubs on the Strip.

TAO Las Vegas

Taqueria Cañonita (Venetian)

Mexican ✕✕

Grand Canal Shoppes, 3377 Las Vegas Blvd. S.

Phone: 702-414-3773
Web: www.canonita.net
Prices: $$

Lunch & dinner daily

Imagine yourself sitting on a stone terrace on the banks of a Venetian canal, enjoying "Mexico City soul food" against a background of Italian arias sung by passing gondoliers. No, you haven't just landed on another planet—you're in Vegas.

Set on the edge of The Venetian's Grand Canal, Taqueria Cañonita's patio makes a great casual place to dine any time of year as it's always sunny underneath the realistic-looking painted sky. Service is informal and friendly, and the waitstaff is happy to offer menu suggestions. Inside, the dining room is decorated with orange accent walls, bright tilework, and Mexican artifacts.

Each dish here is a gourmet experience. The spice is right in a Zacatecas chile relleno; a grilled Michoacan pork chop, served atop creamy mushroom hominy with a pasilla de Oaxaca reduction; and tacos with corn or flour tortillas handmade on-site.

Top of the World (Stratosphere)

American 🍴🍴

B1

2000 Las Vegas Blvd. S.

Phone: 702-380-7711   Lunch & dinner daily
Web: www.topoftheworldlv.com
Prices: $$$

Acrophobics need not apply at this lofty restaurant, which looms 832 feet in the air at the top of the Stratosphere Tower. But if you crave an unparalleled 360-degree view of the Strip in all its glittering glory, you've come to the right place.

You won't find a better vista than at this special-occasion space, where the multicourse menus for two nourish celebrations with the likes of chateaubriand and the signature chocolate Stratosphere for dessert. Don't expect the level of food to match the height of the tower, though; this is a place where view definitely trumps cuisine.

Because Top of the World is so popular with visitors, reservations are recommended for lunch, and required for dinner. A full revolution takes about an hour and twenty minutes to complete, so you won't miss an angle during your meal. All you have to do is sit there … and rotate.

109

Trattoria del Lupo (Mandalay Bay)

Italian 🍴🍴

3950 Las Vegas Blvd. S.

Phone: 702-740-5522   Dinner daily
Web: www.wolfgangpuck.com
Prices: $$$

Wolfgang Puck's casual cafe, set on a stone-lined restaurant row just off the casino floor, evokes an Italian trattoria with its closely clustered tables, pastel colors, antique furnishings, large central bar, and airy indoor patio.

Exhibition pizza, antipasto, and dessert stations give diners a look at the careful technique that marks each straightforward dish here. Bold flavors harmonize equally well in a simple starter of shaved Italian meats, arranged around a ramekin of spicy oil-cured olives, peppers and dried cranberries, or a signature pizza topped with tiger shrimp, braised pancetta and leeks. Pastas are made fresh on the premises.

For dessert, a warm panini of sweet Italian egg bread scented with honey and vanilla and enclosing a filling of creamy, rich hazelnut butter will make you howl with pleasure.

Trevi (Caesars Palace)

Italian ✗✗

B3

The Forum Shops, 3500 Las Vegas Blvd. S.

Phone: 702-735-4663

Lunch & dinner daily

Web: www.trevi-italian.com

Prices: $$

True to its name, a nod to Rome's most famous fountain, this trattoria can be found adjacent to the baroque Fountain of the Gods in the Caesars Forum Shops. Faux-marble figures and thunderous spouts of water provide the ambience for Trevi's indoor mall "patio," furnished with bright mosaic-topped tables and red-cushioned wrought-iron chairs.

Inside, a 12-foot-high orange chandelier made of cascading blown-glass forms the centerpiece of the circular, bi-level dining room. Brick-oven-fired pizzas, specialty pastas (from cappellini *al pomodoro* to linguine with clams) and a selection of entrées, such as hearty chicken parmigiana, will satisfy any appetite.

If you don't have time to dine, you can still grab a pick-me-up from the walk-up gelato/espresso bar. And by all means, throw a coin in the fountain and make a wish to return … just like they do in Rome.

Valentino (Venetian)

Italian XXX

B3

3355 Las Vegas Blvd. S.

Phone: 702-414-3000
Web: www.valentinolv.com
Prices: $$$$

Lunch & dinner daily

Sicilian-born restaurateur Piero Selvaggio runs the Las Vegas satellite of Valentino, whose big sister has been a favorite of Santa Monica diners for more than 30 years. This version of Valentino is divided into two distinct dining areas: the casual and boisterous grill; and beyond, the main dining space—open only for dinner. The latter is refined and intimate, done in a warm contemporary style. Rooms for private parties are lined with displays of bottles from the restaurant's award-winning wine list.

In the kitchen, Executive Chef and partner Luciano Pellegrini fashions a menu that reflects his own Italian heritage. Seasonal dishes (Angus Porterhouse Fiorentina with aged balsamic; monkfish pan-seared in brown butter; and ravioli stuffed with mascarpone cheese and pear in gorgonzola fondue) incorporate products imported from Italy as well as ingredients found stateside.

The Venetian

Verandah (Mandalay Bay)

Contemporary ✗✗✗

A-B5

Four Seasons, 3960 Las Vegas Blvd. S.

Phone: 702-632-5121

Web: www.fourseasons.com/lasvegas

Prices: $$$

Lunch & dinner daily

Like a breezy southern porch, with archways open to the outdoor patio, Verandah conjures up visions of sipping a refreshing iced tea amid leafy palms to stave off the torpid heat.

The L-shaped outdoor terrace, overlooking lush landscaping and the Four Seasons' pool, is the place to lunch—except on searing desert summer days. Seeing all those heavenly bodies by the pool may inspire you to order one of the many light and healthy items. International appeal pervades the lunch fare, from Asian chicken lettuce wraps to a Niçoise tuna salad. At dinnertime, the menu moves to Italy, transported by choices such as rustic lasagna, lobster ravioli with spinach and leeks, and red-wine-braised short ribs. Verandah also serves breakfast and an oh-so-civilized afternoon tea (Monday through Thursday).

Soft greens and warm woods in the indoor room enhance the Mediterranean feel.

Wing Lei ❀ (Wynn)

B2

Chinese XXXX

The Strip

3131 Las Vegas Blvd. S.

Phone: 702-248-3463
Web: www.wynnlasvegas.com
Prices: $$$$

Dinner daily

&

The seduction begins the minute you enter Wing Lei, with its exotic dining room dressed in glimmering glass, dark wood lattice, and gold accents. Outside, a garden boasts century-old pomegranate trees and a black marble Botero sculpture. And yet it's Chef Richard Chen's haute Chinese menu that remains the focus, with its heady mix of Cantonese, Shanghai, and Sichuan specialties.

Peking duck, along with Chen's artful seafood creations, are the main attraction for dinner—start with plump, fresh prawns, pan-sautéed in a sweet red chili sauce, and served with a handful of *choy sum* stalks; and then move on to a whole Peking duck, which is carved tableside and folded into thin crepes laced with hoisin sauce, crunchy cucumber, and scallions.

Save room for a dessert of decadent little white chocolate truffles, oozing with mousses and sorbets, and garnished with gold leaves.

Appetizers	*Entrées*	*Desserts*
• Shrimp, Green Papaya Salad, Chili, Fish Vinaigrette	• Pan-seared Scallops, Shimeji Mushrooms, Green Beans	• Baked Brioche, Pastry Cream, Vanilla Ice Cream, Hot Fudge Sauce
• B.B.Q. Ribs, Spice-Soy Reduction, Pickled Cabbage	• Wok-fried Australian Lobster, Bamboo Shoots, Shiitake	• Hazelnut Cake with Caramelized Hazelnut Candy, Hazelnut Ice Cream
• Poached Lobster, Lemongrass Sauce	• Wok-fried Kobe Beef, Shishito Pepper, Shaoxing	• Red Bean Crème Brûlée

Yellowtail (Bellagio)

Japanese XX

B3

3600 Las Vegas Blvd. S.

Phone: 702-730-3900
Web: www.bellagio.com
Prices: $$$$

Dinner daily

Nothing stays the same in Vegas for very long, as this newcomer to Bellagio proves. Taking over the space formerly occupied by Shintaro, Yellowtail looks out over Lake Bellagio from the balcony of its marble patio. At the lakeside tables you'll be misted by water from the dramatic fountain shows. Wood, stone, and bronze metal sculptures fashion a contemporary space inside.

Sushi, sashimi, and maki are admittedly pricey, but also better than much of the Japanese fare found in Vegas. For the most innovative offerings, go for the omakase. Fresh ingredients flown in from afar determine your feast: perhaps a cylinder of yellowtail tartare stacked in a pool of wasabi-spiked soy sauce; salmon sashimi sparked by a sweet miso glaze; and the signature Big Time Roll, with its decadent filling of King crab and asparagus, wrapped in thin slices of Kobe beef and slices of black truffle.

The Light Group

Zine (Palazzo)

B2

Asian 🍴

3325 Las Vegas Blvd. S.

Phone: 702-607-2220
Web: www.palazzolasvegas.com
Prices: $$$

Lunch & dinner daily

One of the restaurants gracing the new Palazzo hotel, this casual-chic gem wins big with tourists, families, and hotel guests alike. The restaurant—located right off the main casino floor—is open from lunchtime to late night, making it a convenient spot for a meal most any time.

Diners definitely don't go away hungry here. Generously sized dishes look mainly to China for their inspiration, but the menu draws on an array of other Asian cooking styles as well. Bold flavors ring out in dim sum such as Shanghai-style pork dumplings, and chicken in spicy sesame sauce; while chef's specials like Singapore-style pan-fried chili crab served in a pool of piquant broth makes a messy but memorable meal. In this kitchen, even fried rice reaches high notes with bits of salty dried white fish, tender strips of chicken, and an assortment of vegetables scented with ginger and sesame oil.

Innovation
for the future

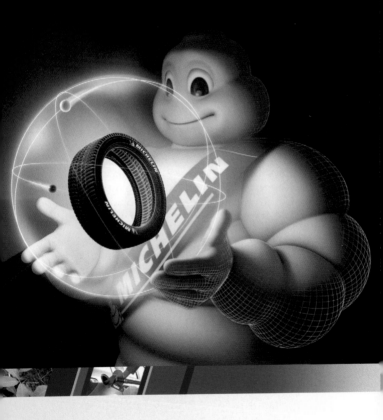

www.michelin.com

East of The Strip

It's business, brains, and basketball east of The Strip, between the commercial district, Las Vegas Convention Center, McCarran International Airport, and the University of Nevada at Las Vegas (UNLV). Some newer casinos and non-gaming hotels are located here as well, but many locals favor the smaller, less glitzy places on the old Boulder Strip. To abandon the neon altogether head for **Lake Mead**, the largest man-made lake in the U.S. Created by the damming of the Colorado River during the construction of Hoover Dam. Lake Mead now forms part of a national recreation area offering 1-1/2-million acres of outdoor fun.

Modern Casinos

Between The Strip and Lake Mead, **Henderson** is Nevada's second-largest and one of America's fastest-growing cities. Once a working-class factory town in the desert, it's now a place of placid waters and pastoral pleasures attracting the affluent to its planned communities. Green Valley was the first, setting the pace with its verdant

landscaping, golf courses, and shopping complexes. Family-friendliness and wholesome recreation aside, this is still Vegas. Green Valley is home to one of the area's luxurious casino resorts, Green Valley Ranch. On nearby **Lake Las Vegas**, you'll find other opulent casinos and lodgings, along with more world-class golf courses, fine dining, and high-end shopping—all in a setting that's more like Tuscany than the desert.

Ancient Cultures

Twenty miles farther to the southeast is Sin City's polar opposite. **Boulder City** was built in 1929 to accommodate **Hoover Dam** workers and their families. There's plenty of charm but not a slot machine to be had in Nevada's only gambling-free town. The engineering marvel that Boulder City's citizens built down the road, however, spurred Las Vegas's gaming industry after the railroad left Vegas behind.

A visit to Overton, on Lake Mead's north end, will remind you that long before neon, nature and native cultures performed dazzling feats here. The **Lost City Museum** houses artifacts of people who dwelled in the cliffs 1,000 years ago. Visitors can admire their petroglyphs, as well as the red sandstone formations created by wind and water during the Jurassic Period, at **Valley of Fire State Park.**

Ago (Hard Rock)

Italian XXX

B3

4455 Paradise Rd.

Phone: 702-693-4440
Web: www.hardrockhotel.com
Prices: $$$

Dinner daily

In early 2008, Chef Agostino Sciandri stepped in where Chef Kerry Simon stepped out at the Hard Rock Hotel. Sciandri, along with partner Robert DeNiro, marked the tenth anniversary of the original Los Angeles location of his eponymous restaurant by opening this outpost in the desert.

Importing the flavors of his native Tuscany to the distinctly warmer Las Vegas clime, Chef Sciandri's heritage shines in dishes such as pan-roasted quail with stewed lentils and *lardo*; pappardelle with wild boar ragù; and potato-wrapped turbot served with a tapenade-style relish bursting with ripe olive flavor.

A large welcoming lounge makes a primo spot in which to sip a glass of Chianti or Primitivo before being seated in the airy, casual dining room, with its warm gold tones and potted palms. Once the sun sets, mesh curtains are pulled back to reveal views of the hotel pool.

Hard Rock Hotel & Casino

A.J.'s Steakhouse (Hard Rock)

Steakhouse ✗✗✗

B3

4455 Paradise Rd.

Tue – Sat dinner only

Phone: 702-693-5500
Web: www.hardrockhotel.com
Prices: $$

From a prime burger to a hefty 22-ounce bone-in ribeye, the menu here can accommodate a range of hungry carnivores. Aromas of searing meat waft from the open kitchen, sparking appetites for grilled steaks and chops cooked in classic style.

Sides highlight steakhouse staples, like roasted fingerling potatoes, creamed spinach, sautéed broccolini, or wedges of iceberg lettuce with blue cheese salad, and are priced à la carte. Flavorful and tender shrimp scampi or Maine lobster cater to those who prefer seafood.

Nostalgia abounds in the elegant retro décor, which hearkens back to the Rat Pack era in Vegas when several rounds of martinis topped off by a cigarette was considered a meal—a pleasant diversion from the Gen X hipsters stirring through the rest of the casino. Every night, a piano man tickles the ivories, making diners swoon in homage to bygone crooners.

121

Bistro Zinc

American 🍴

G3

15 Via Bel Canto, Henderson

Phone: 702-567-9462
Web: www.bistrozincrestaurant.com
Prices: $$

Wed – Sun lunch & dinner
Mon – Tue dinner only

Chef/owner Joseph Keller (brother to renowned Chef Thomas Keller) hits high notes with his jazzy French-Cajun riff on American cuisine at this causal restaurant in MonteLago Village. The façade styles a Tuscan villa, but the ambience and interior décor fashions a French bistro with a zinc counter, raw bar, and cane-back bentwood chairs.

Daily specials are chalked on a blackboard, complementing menu items such as the Parisienne filet burger; Maryland crab cake served with homemade tropical salsa; free-range chicken pot pie; and Atlantic halibut meunière. Fresh seafood is flown in every day, while many of the vegetables and herbs come from the on-site garden.

For a refreshing vista on a warm day, grab a seat on the outdoor terrace overlooking the lake. This also makes the perfect perch to catch the seasonal jazz concerts presented in the village on Friday nights.

Firefly

Spanish ✗

B3

3900 Paradise Rd. (bet. Corporate Dr. & E. Twain Ave.)

Lunch & dinner daily

Phone: 702-369-3971
Web: www.fireflylv.com
Prices: ◌◌

A hip place for a light and casual meal, Firefly makes its home just east of the Strip on busy Paradise Road. The extended kitchen hours (until 3:00 A.M. Friday and Saturday; 2:00 A.M. other nights) appeal to the twenty-something set who flits to this tapas bar for late-night snacking.

Small plates include an extensive array of hot and cold choices such as vegetable empanadas; hearty tortilla *a la española* omelet filled with potatoes, onions, and garlic; gazpacho; and *boquerones* toasts topped with white Spanish anchovies. A few larger plates and entrees, such as steak frites or herb-roasted chicken, complete the menu.

Liven the party with a refreshing pitcher of red or white sangria served over diced apples and ice, then lose yourself to the beat of the Latin music. Come for the clubby atmosphere, the minimalist chic décor, and enjoy a multicourse meal at off-the-Strip prices.

Gandhi

Indian

B3

4080 Paradise Rd. (at Flamingo Rd.)

Phone: 702-734-0094
Web: www.gandhicuisine.com
Prices:

Lunch & dinner daily

Savvy Las Vegas diners can take an inexpensive epicurean tour through Kolcata, Kashmir, and Mumbai simply by walking through an unassuming glass door, tucked behind Morton's Steakhouse in a little strip mall. Inside, you may be surprised to find an airy, spacious room with mezzanine seating and softly playing Indian music buffered by an enormous, sprawling tapestry suspended from the lofty ceiling. Lunchtime choices are limited to the buffet, but no one complains when they discover this affordable and bounteous array of northern and southern Indian dishes. This is an ideal opportunity for diners less familiar with the cuisine to acquaint themselves with the likes of perfectly seasoned tandoori chicken or fresh, flavorful papadom and naan breads. Dinners offer a full menu of specialities that include seafood delicacies, tongue-tingling curries, and extensive vegetarian options.

Hank's Fine Steaks & Martinis
(Green Valley Ranch)

Steakhouse

F4

2300 Paseo Verde Pkwy., Henderson

Dinner daily

Phone: 702-617-7515
Web: www.greenvalleyranchresort.com
Prices: $$$$

Named for journalist, Green Valley developer, and controversial local icon Hank Greenspun (1909-1989), Hank's lures both locals and guests at ritzy Green Valley Ranch (*see hotel listing*). Upon arriving, allow yourself to be drawn to the backlit onyx bar for one of the 30 different martinis—classic or creative, they are consistently well-made. Pass through the piano lounge, to enter the glamorous dining room, bedecked with crystal chandeliers sparkling over dark wood, leather-upholstered chairs and gray-blue booths—all invoking an updated late-40s Vegas ambience.

The cuisine conjures the same era, shining its spotlight on prime, corn-fed, dry-aged beef, with seafood items peppering the menu. Sides are à la carte and can add dearly to the total, but those interested in throwing caution to the wind should top their steaks with a slice of seared foie gras.

Hofbräuhaus

German ✗

4510 Paradise Rd. (at Harmon Ave.)

Phone: 702-853-2337
Web: www.hofbrauhauslasvegas.com
Prices: ⬤⬤

Lunch & dinner daily

Seekers of high-spirited dining—and drinking—will find a home here. An exact reproduction of Hofbräuhaus München, commissioned by Duke Wilhelm V in 1589, this lively restaurant re-creates an authentic German beer hall.

There is seating for some 800 diners, between the *Schwemme* (beer hall) and the temperature-controlled *biergarten*, but long, wooden, communal tables bring strangers together in perpetual celebration of Oktoberfest. Order a liter of the rich, amber *Oktoberfest* ale or dark *Dunkel brau* along with a fresh soft pretzel from a waitress clad in Bavarian garb, then sing along with the German band that entertains diners nightly.

Bavarian specialties such as tender pork loin chops and links of smokey sausages accompanied by traditional sauerkraut leave guests sated but happy. Be sure to save room for the delicately layered, delicious apple strudel.

India Palace

Indian ✕

C3

505 E. Twain Ave. (bet. Paradise Rd. & Swenson St.)

Phone: 702-796-4177
Web: N/A
Prices: 💲💲

Lunch & dinner daily

Do not let the exterior of India Palace deter you from visiting this fine restaurant. The daily lunch buffet is famous among locals; stacks of plates near the entrance invite diners to sample an extravaganza of exotic fare at a bargain price. Dishes are labeled to assist novices of Indian food, but half the fun is experimenting with new flavors. From mild to spicy, all the offerings are worth this venture east of the more glamorous, high-profile places on the Strip.

The dinner menu remains reasonably priced, with entrées featuring pronounced spices and exotic seasonings. Crisp, creamy, zesty, tangy, and tender represent the gamut of flavors to be found in dishes of biryani rice, curries, tandoori oven-baked dinners, and *tikka masala* (meat or fish simmered in fresh tomato sauce), as well as an ample list of vegetarian options.

Kilawat (Platinum)

Contemporary XXX

B3

211 E. Flamingo Rd.
Phone: 702-636-2525
Web: www.theplatinumhotel.com
Prices: $$$

Tue – Sat lunch & dinner
Sun – Mon lunch only

Formerly the restaurant at Platinum, this urbane and romantic dining room has been recharged with a new name, a new chef, and a new menu. Kilawat is set on the fifth floor of the non-gaming, non-smoking, all-suites Platinum Hotel (*see hotel listing*), where it looks out on the hotel pool through a wall of glass.

Contemporary American touches shine through in the carefully prepared cuisine. "Sizzle" with fried curried chicken croquettes; experience "synergy" with all-inclusive entrées like citrus barbecue-glazed salmon plated alongside warm German-style potatoes and organic greens; or pick your own "components" from a list of meats, fish, sauces, and sides.

Since the hotel is set off the beaten Strip track, Kilawat will need to prove itself as a destination restaurant in order to succeed. Only time will tell if this establishment will be something that stays in Vegas.

Lindo Michoacán

Mexican ✗

E2

2655 E. Desert Inn Rd. (bet. McLeod Dr. & S. Eastern Ave.)
Lunch & dinner daily

Phone: 702-735-6828
Web: www.lindomichoacancatering.com
Prices: $$

Playfully decorated with colorful paintings, Mexican masks, and a bar flanked by shelf after shelf of tequila, Lindo Michoacán raises the stakes on Mexican food in Las Vegas. Here, Chef/owner Javier Barajas appeals to a varied audience with an extensive menu of tried-and-true classics as well as more adventurous preparations.

Those playing it safe can enjoy standards like *huevos rancheros*, tacos, and enchiladas; but riskier Vegas visitors have ample opportunity for something authentic and different, such as the grilled Mexican cactus. Specialties include the signature steak in Coca-Cola sauce, made according to Mama Consuelo's secret recipe. A large selection of lunch specials and combinations are modestly priced.

Since Barajas' doctor put him on a heart-healthy diet, he has forsaken the lard traditionally used in Mexican cooking; thus only vegetable and olive oils are used.

©Mark Gibson

Lotus of Siam

Thai ✗

953 E. Sahara Ave. (bet. Maryland Pkwy & Paradise Rd.)

Phone: 702-735-3033
Web: www.saipinchutima.com
Prices: **$$**

Mon – Fri lunch & dinner
Sat – Sun dinner only

Vibrant, exotic flavors of Thai cuisine compensate for what this strip-mall restaurant lacks in terms of ambience. The décor mainly features framed photos of staff with random patrons and the occasional celebrity dotting the walls. Still, a coterie of regulars and in-the-know visitors pack the midday buffet lunch (a full à la carte menu is also available).

One menu focuses on northern Thailand, so these items are milder in spice than those from other regions of the country, with strong influences from Laos, Myanmar, and the Hunan province of south China. In addition, Chef/owner Saipin Chutima has also fashioned a second standard menu to be a virtual encyclopedia of Thai favorites from barbecue chicken to mild yellow curry. Add to that daily specials such as deep-fried sea bass with "drunken noodles" and the challenge here may be narrowing down your choices.

Jakrapan Atcharawan

Lucille's Smokehouse Barbeque

Barbecue ✗

F4

2245 Village Walk Dr. (at Paseo Verde Pkwy.), Henderson
Lunch & dinner daily

Phone: 702-257-7427
Web: www.lucillesbbq.com
Prices: $$

Those who tire of fancy food and seek a laid-back, soulful desert retreat will be right at home at this California-based barbecue chain founded by Lucille Buchanan. Inside, the décor hollers roadhouse with linoleum floors, red vinyl booths, and mismatched chairs spread throughout several rooms. Enclosed country-style porches with lazy ceiling fans lend touches of genuine Americana.

Tap your toes to the rhythm-and-blues while chowing down southern specialties such as New Orleans gumbo, pan-blackened catfish, and braised Angus short ribs. However, this is serious barbecue; chicken, pork, and beef are all slow-smoked over hickory, served with homemade biscuits and, of course, smoky-sweet house sauce.

Silverware is provided, although this food begs to be eaten with fingers—warm, moist towels are presented to clean your saucy paws when finished.

Marrakech

Moroccan 🍽

B3

3900 Paradise Rd. (at Corporate Dr.)

Phone: 702-737-5611
Web: N/A
Prices: $$

Dinner daily

♿

A short drive east of the Strip to a Paradise Road mall offers an exotic Morrocan outpost where tent-like fabric billows from the dining-room ceiling and colored-glass lanterns cast a sexy glow over luxurious tapestries, copper urns, and blue-tiled archways.

Since 1979, this desert oasis has been serving traditional, beautifully-presented Moroccan feasts in abundance. Meals are served family-style and are customarily eaten without utensils (forks and knives are available upon request). Sink into a low-lying banquette, listen to the upbeat north African music, and begin a transporting meal with a hummus and babaganoush platter, featuring spiced and pickled vegetables alongside wedges of pita that combine to highlight true Mediterranean flavors. A sweetened take on *b'stilla*, the flaky Moroccan pie traditionally made with squab, is accompanied by mint tea for dessert.

©Mark Gibon

Marssa (Loews)

Asian ✗✗

G2

101 Montelago Blvd., Henderson

Mon – Sat dinner only

Phone: 702-567-6000
Web: www.loewshotels.com
Prices: $$$

An Asian oasis in the midst of an otherwise Moroccan-inspired atmosphere, Marssa is the fine-dining option at the Loews Lake Las Vegas Resort *(see hotel listing)*. (It was formerly called Japengo when the hotel was a Hyatt.) *Marssa* means "by the sea," in this case the Pacific Rim—which inspires an exciting menu that emphasizes, but is not limited to, seafood.

Sichuan pepper beef noodles in garlic chile broth sounds intriguing, but the serious sushi is hard to pass up. *Opakapaka lau lau*, Hawaiian snapper wrapped in banana leaves with coconut ginger sauce, kabocha squash and banana chutney exemplifies the exotic offerings that show a deft and delectable balance of assertive flavors.

Refined service and elegant touches such as orchids, candlelight and Asian-inspired china complement the artfully presented cuisine, as do the comprehensive wine and sake lists.

Medici Café (Ritz-Carlton Lake Las Vegas)

G3

Contemporary ✗✗✗

1610 Lake Las Vegas Pkwy., Henderson

Phone: 702-567-4700

Web: www.ritz-carlton.com

Prices: $$$$

Lunch & dinner daily

Housed in the Ritz-Carlton Lake Las Vegas, Medici visually lives up to its noble Tuscan name. The lovely terrace looks onto the hotel's manicured Florentine garden, just beyond which is a performance space where musicians entertain on warm evenings. Italianate dark wood furnishings and reproductions of Renaissance art grace the interior. More a princely dining retreat than a formal hall, the space is comfortably elegant. It's just right for another kind of renaissance reflected in the display kitchen and its contemporary American menu.

Incorporating great seasonal ingredients, dishes here combine complementary flavors that the Medici surely would have enjoyed: a velvety sweet potato bisque enhanced by a swirl of chipotle cream; and a well-marbled filet mignon plated beside a scoop of caramelized-onion risotto, balanced by the slight bitterness of wilted greens.

Nobu ❀ (Hard Rock)

Japanese ✕✕

B3

4455 Paradise Rd.

Phone: 702-693-5090   Dinner daily
Web: www.hardrockhotel.com
Prices: $$$$

Hard Rock Hotel

Famed Chef Nobu Matsuhisa's Vegas baby is a sleek looker housed on the lobby level of the Hard Rock Hotel. Most evenings, the beautiful Japanese-inspired room is thumping with music and teeming with young, stylish types—but the upbeat staff keeps the crowds in check with casual, polished service.

Nobu's signature miso black cod graces the Japanese-with-a-hint-of-South-American menu; as well as a host of small plates, sushi, sashimi, and the like—with many of the ingredients flown in fresh from Tokyo. Start with a live Japanese scallop, opened to order and quickly cut into silky, tissue-thin slices. Fanned back into its shell with English cucumber and garnished with yuzu juice, the result is spectacular. Move on to barely-seared slices of delicate Washu beef tataki, dancing in a tangy ponzu sauce and dusted with cracked pepper, then garnished with micro greens.

Appetizers	*Entrées*	*Desserts*
• Spicy Miso "Chips" with Tuna or Scallops • Yellowtail Sashimi with Jalapeño • Mixed Seafood Ceviche	• Black Cod with Miso • Chilean Sea Bass with Black Bean Sauce or Dried Miso • Rock Shrimp Tempura with Butter Ponzu or Creamy Spicy Sauce	• Bento Box • Hibiscus Champagne Cocktail • Chestnut, Chocolate and Pears

Origin India

C3

Indian 🍴🍴

4480 Paradise Rd. (at Harmon Rd.)

Phone: 702-734-6342
Web: www.originindiarestaurant.com
Prices: $$

Lunch & dinner daily

Leave the Strip behind to savor the bold, fresh flavors at Origin India. Delicious northern and southern Indian classics consistently earn top billing on the local "best of" lists. This talent and skill is exemplified in such dishes as *chana masala* of buttery chickpeas stewed with onion, garlic, ginger, and pungent Indian spices, tempered by slices of fresh cucumber and creamy yogurt; or a traditional lamb curry that awakens taste buds with its blend of fiery spices. Served hot and crisp from the tandoor oven, lightly brushed with clarified butter, *naan* is the perfect accompaniment to any meal.

Located in a strip mall facing the Hard Rock Hotel, this modern restaurant features dark tinted windows to prevent curious eyes from peering in. High-backed leather chairs and wrought-iron light fixtures create a chic ambience, while curtained alcoves provide intimate niches for private dining.

Pasta Shop & Ristorante

Italian ✗

E3

2495 E. Tropicana Ave. (bet. S. Eastern Ave. & Topaz St.)

Dinner daily

Phone: 702-451-1893
Web: www.pastashop.com
Prices: $$

Upstate New York natives and brothers David (the chef) and Glenn Alenik (the manager) combined their culinary and business backgrounds to open a pasta shop and restaurant in 1988. Loyal regulars are greeted by name at this strip-mall eatery, where fresh pasta by the pound is available to take home.

A Caesar salad and garlic bread accompany the locally renowned handmade pastas such as a traditional, creamy fettucine Alfredo, or more daring and harmonious creations such as the saffron shrimp sauté with squid-ink fettuccini. Other offerings focus on simple and savory classics like eggplant parmesan, chicken Marsala, and a selection of brick-oven-baked pizzas.

Here, old-world charm is fostered by friendly service and a chic interior design that punctuates the dining room's zebra-patterned table clothes and yellow walls with eclectic art, most of which is for sale.

Piero's

B2

Italian ✗✗✗

355 Convention Center Dr. (at Paradise Rd.)

Phone: 702-369-2305
Web: www.pieroscuisine.com
Prices: $$

Dinner daily

Founded by Freddie Glusman in 1982, this old-style Vegas restaurant has been in its present location across from the Las Vegas Convention Center since 1986. Here, it lures a steady stream of conventioneers and notables (a list of celebrity patrons is posted, if you're interested) who come for the likes of crispy fried calamari, tender osso buco, and spinach-stuffed *agnollotti alla crema* delivered by white-tuxedo-clad waiters.

Piero's, with its Aldo Luongo lithographs, original oil paintings and tiger-striped carpeting, stood in for one of the Mob hangouts in Martin Scorsese's 1995 film *Casino*. Despite the restaurant's generous size (nine separate dining rooms can seat 345 diners), it's best to make reservations as the place fills up quickly. If you do decide to drop in on a busy night, try for first-come, first-served seating at one of the black-granite bars.

Piero's

Pink Taco (Hard Rock)

Mexican ✗

4455 Paradise Rd.

Phone: 702-693-5525
Web: www.hardrockhotel.com
Prices: $$

Lunch & dinner daily

Strewn with *mucho* Mexican folk art and kitchy paraphernalia, this festive cantina in the Hard Rock Hotel *(see hotel listing)* is the place to party at happy hour (Monday through Friday from 4:00-7:00 P.M.). Slam down two-for-one *cervezas* and house margaritas along with half-price appetizers.

Yet reasons to come here extend beyond the bar specials and highly suggestive name—yes, there really is a pink taco (*panuchos*), stuffed with beans and topped with grilled chicken, salsa *roja*, pickled onions, and avocado. Start with crisp tortilla chips accompanied by a trio of fresh and spicy salsas while perusing the menu. Selections include burritos and tacos, but also highlight *platos fuertes* (hot dishes), such as achiote-grilled chicken breast, chipotle-glazed salmon, and the *chilaquiles* casserole of roasted vegetables. Watch the fresh corn tortillas being made while waiting for your meal.

Hard Rock Hotel

Settebello

F4

1776 Horizon Ridge Pkwy. (at Valley Verde Dr.), Henderson

Lunch & dinner daily

Phone: 702-222-3556
Web: www.settebello.net
Prices: ⊗⊗

Outside Italy, this is one of the most authentic Neapolitan-style pizzas around. Settebello is one on a short list of pizzerias in the U.S. to be certified by the VPN (Verace Pizza Napoletana), the association charged with preserving the art of this treasured food heritage.

The main attraction of this spot is the wood-burning pizza oven, imported from Italy and assembled painstakingly piece-by-piece.

The pizza makers are dedicated and passionate in their craft of individual-size pies. The perfectly charred crusts, topped with imported Italian tomatoes and mozzarella are simply delicious. Fresh toppings create sensational combinations in specialties like the Settebello, topped with pancetta, fennel sausage, roasted mushrooms, pine nuts, mozzarella, basil, and olive oil.

Settebello is moving to a new location in The District at Green Valley Ranch.

Settebello

SushiWa

E4

790 Coronado Center Dr. (at Eastern Ave.), Henderson

Phone: 702-263-5785
Web: N/A
Prices: $$

Mon – Sat lunch & dinner
Sun dinner

Looking to escape the never-ending crush of tourists along the Strip? Check out SushiWa for some serious off-Strip action—of the culinary kind. You won't find many tourists here; this Henderson hangout is a local favorite for good-quality sushi and specialty rolls.

Served attractively on an oblong platter, straight-forward sushi such as slices of tuna, salmon, white fish, and shrimp nigiri are punctuated with mounds of sticky rice and wasabi paste. A spicy tuna roll is filled with rice and batons of cucumber, and cut into neat mouth-sized pieces. For those who shudder at the thought of raw seafood, hot dishes run the gamut from miso-marinated Chilean sea bass to a Kobe beef plate.

Down-to-earth shades of gray and brown combine with natural materials (wood floors, stacked stone walls, and leather chairs) to form a pleasant setting that belies its humble strip-mall location.

SushiWa

Table 34

American ✗

East of The Strip

E4

600 E. Warm Springs Rd. (at Amigo St.)

Phone: 702-263-0034
Web: N/A
Prices: **$$$**

Tue – Fri lunch & dinner
Sat dinner only
Mon lunch only

Just south of the airport, Table 34 is no secret to locals, who pack the place at both lunch and dinner. Warm merlot and sage hues add color to the otherwise plain room. The waitstaff greets many of the regulars by name, and the service is friendly and attentive—even during the lunch rush.

Tradition may dictate the well-prepared American dishes, but the ingredients and execution here rank well above the norm. At lunch, sandwiches (a French dip with caramelized shallots, gruyère, and thyme jus), pasta (linguine with chicken, spinach, and tomatoes in garlic cream), and pizzas constitute the bulk of the menu. The evening meal rolls out a longer list of main courses like a crispy seared salmon served atop a bed of cauliflower purée, and then drizzled with a lemon-juice-infused beurre blanc to give it a classic touch.

Expect to wait for a table or sit at the bar if you're going solo.

Table 34

Terra Verde (Green Valley Ranch)

Italian ✗✗

F4

2300 Paseo Verde Pkwy., Henderson

Phone:	702-617-7777	Mon – Sat dinner only
Web:	www.greenvalleyranchresort.com	Sun lunch & dinner
Prices:	$$$	

Newcomer to the Green Valley Ranch resort *(see hotel listing)*, Terra Verde has garnered notoriety of late as the restaurant where *Hell's Kitchen* contestant Rock Harper landed after winning the popular FOX network cooking competition. Television personalities aside, this spacious Italian eatery—tucked into a corner off the casino floor—merits a visit for its flavorful Italian dishes.

The cavernous space, decked out with warm wood paneling, soft lighting, and French doors opening onto outdoor dining terraces, has clearly become a dining destination for Henderson residents.

Attentive, amiable, and unwaveringly professional, the service alone is enough to bring you back. Poached Mediterranean sea bass bathed in a pool of tomato-garlic broth; and pan-seared veal *involtini* (rolled with prosciutto, fontina, sage, and spinach) speak volumes about the talent in the kitchen.

Todd's Unique Dining

F u s i o n ✗

F3

4350 E. Sunset Rd. (bet. Anthenian Dr.
& Green Valley Pkwy.), Henderson

Phone: 702-259-8633 Mon – Sat dinner only
Web: www.toddsunique.com
Prices: $$

♿ Not wanting to tie himself down to any one cuisine, Chef Todd Clore labels his strip-mall restaurant menu "unique," combining this, that, and whatever he forages at the market that morning. Malaysian barbecue shrimp with cucumber salad and Johnny cakes; New England clam chowder; Kobe skirt steak grilled with spicy black bean and chile sauce; or an herb-roasted Sonoma chicken may comprise a day's fare. The menu changes daily, so know the ingredients are fresh, well-prepared, and, somehow, harmonious. No matter the country of inspiration, everything travels very well together on the plates.

The small bar area is equipped with a television so neighborhood denizens can hang out and route for their favorite team. Booth seating is cozier opposite the bar, although the décor generally leaves something to be desired. Those in a hurry should drop by early; Todd's opens at 4:30 P.M. for dinner.

Todd Clore/Todds Unique Dining

West of The Strip

Glitter and excitement spill over west of The Strip in popular casino resorts and a host of good restaurants (some located in resorts, some freestanding or in little strip malls). The west side is also home to several hotels for budget-minded tourists who don't mind walking the few extra steps to the casinos to lose the money they're saving on lodging. Yet you don't have to go very far west of The Strip to leave it behind completely for the real West. Not half an hour's drive away is **Red Rock Canyon National Conservation Area**, the Spring Mountains, and a vastly different kind of wild from the perpetual party along Las Vegas Boulevard.

The Wild West...

There is civilization out here. The suburb of **Summerlin** is one of the area's premier planned communities and home to a performing-arts center, a regional professional dance troupe, two championship golf courses, and enough shopping options to ensure that nobody runs out of upscale trail supplies. But the trails—and the hiking, horseback riding, camping,

and rock climbing—are the real draws out here. Along with the scenery, that is. The 3,000-foot-high, 13-mile-long escarpment at **Red Rock Canyon**, which resulted when two geological plates bumped up against each other some 65 million years ago, looks as though a master artist painted bands of gray, red, and white along its sandstone façade. Besides the 30 miles of trails, there's a 13-mile scenic driving loop for those who prefer to experience nature in air-conditioned comfort.

...And The Wilder West

At nearby **Spring Mountain Ranch State Park**, you can visit the ranch once owned by Howard Hughes as well as a campsite used by 19th-century travelers. Imagine traveling back in time and encountering a gunslinger, or joining a posse at **Old Nevada**—a re-created 1880s-era mining town on Bonnie Springs Ranch. And if the desert heat begins to be too much for you, head for the wilderness of the Humboldt-Toiyabe National Forest in the **Spring Mountains National Recreation Area**. Mount Charleston, its highest peak at 12,000 feet, is usually 20 to 40 degrees cooler than Las Vegas.

Las Vegas News Bureau/LVCVA

Alizé ✿ (Palms)

A3

French 🍴🍴🍴

4321 W. Flamingo Rd.

Phone: 702-951-7000
Web: www.alizelv.com
Prices: $$$$

Dinner daily

♿
🍇

The spoiling begins with the private elevator, which whisks you 56 floors above the crash and thrum of the Palms casino, up to a lofty perch at the top of the hotel. Welcome to Alizé—an elegant dining room where the walls double as windows. And if the views of the glimmering lights of downtown Las Vegas aren't intoxicating enough, the contemporary French food courtesy of Chef André Rochat, will surely do the trick.

Try the perfectly seared filet mignon, studded with cracked green peppercorns, draped in a velvety cognac cream, and sided with a sumptuous truffle potato croquette; or fresh sea bass, sautéed in garlic and white wine, and served with hearts of palm salad, beluga lentils, and Manila clams.

After dinner, linger over a glass of wine and a soft slice of cheesecake, laced with a rich huckleberry sauce. Between that and the view, it doesn't get much better.

Appetizers
- Smoked Salmon Parfait, Hackleback Caviar, Buckwheat Blini
- Chilled Australian Rock Lobster Tail with Black Truffles
- Warm Duck Confit, Black Truffle and Spinach Salad

Entrées
- Duck Breast and Cherry-stuffed Duck Leg, Orange-Shallot Sauce
- Rack of Lamb, Fondant Potatoes, Leek Jus
- Veal Loin Medallions, Sweetbreads, Green Onion Fondue

Desserts
- Roasted Peach, Honey-Almond Strudel Cigars
- Milk Chocolate Candy Bar, Smoked Vanilla Ice Cream
- "Banana Split"

Antonio's (Rio)

Italian XXX

A3

3700 W. Flamingo Rd.

Dinner daily

Phone: 702-777-7923
Web: www.harrahs.com
Prices: $$$

Just off the casino floor of Rio's Ipanema Tower is this serene Italian restaurant. A quaint bar area near the entrance beckons patrons with glasses of Barolo or Barbaresco. In the romantic dining room, intimate guests in cozy booths co-exist peacefully with more festive groups, all under a dramatic, domed ceiling painted as a blue sky mural.

Antonio's interprets northern Italian traditions with a gourmet touch, as in the flavorful and pleasing perciatelli pasta tossed with thinly sliced beef tenderloin, candied walnuts, and gorgonzola cream sauce. Enjoy watching the open kitchen expertly prepare and present their satisfying *pesce* specialties like crisp branzino, or *carne* offerings as such as herb-crusted grilled veal Porterhouse or Pine Valley Ranch double-cut lamb chops.

Remember to order Antonio's signature soufflé during dinner—it takes 25 minutes to prepare.

Archi's Thai Kitchen

Thai 🍴

E2

6360 W. Flamingo Rd. (at Torrey Pines Dr.)

Phone: 702-880-5550

Web: N/A

Prices: 🍥

Tue – Sun lunch & dinner

A little diamond in the rough (meaning strip mall), Archi's is an unexpected treasure on the west side of Vegas. Expect authentic Thai cuisine and a spice level that may exceed American tastes; request the degree of heat you desire—from 1 to 10 (inducing tears)—and the chefs will gladly comply.

Service is basic and the décor looks a bit the worse for wear, but this neighborhood gem attracts crowds of local business types who gather for fresh Thai food at bargain prices. Excellent, low-cost lunch combinations include a choice of specified entrées served with soup, rice, and egg rolls. At dinner, à la carte offerings show more ambition in flavor and cooking technique, as in the Panang curry in coconut sauce or spicy eggplant sautéed with chile and garlic sauce. Accompany any meal with a refreshing and traditional chrysanthemum-infused Thai iced-tea.

DJT ❀ (Trump International Hotel & Tower)

Contemporary 🍴🍴🍴🍴

2000 Fashion Show Dr.

Phone:	702-476-7358
Web:	www.trumplasvegashotel.com
Prices:	$$$$

Tue – Sun dinner only

Located in the shiny new Trump hotel, DJT couldn't want for better digs. Even the walk to the restaurant—with uniformed bellmen ushering you in like royalty—is set to impress. And then there's DJT itself, which boasts a sexy but refined space, dressed in deep purple walls and filled with intimate little curtained alcoves for super romantic dining.

But what's even more exciting is the fact that behind the shiny new package is a very solid kitchen—with Executive Chef Joe Isidori spinning a thoroughly inventive modern menu touched with Asian components. A moist, flaky halibut arrives prepared *sous vide*, sided with a delicious mix of sweet pea tortellini, sautéed crawfish, and a sliced roulade of sweetbreads and mousseline; while a roasted Florida cobia gets paired with caponata-stuffed squid and lemony razor clams wrapped in tender, smoky eggplant.

Appetizers

- Chilled Sweet Pea Soup with Fromage Blanc, Fruit and Vegetable Jewels
- Chilled Lobster with Miso, Cilantro, Apricot
- Roasted Squab with Chinese Black Bean, Tom's Tangerines

Entrées

- Sea Trout with Steel Head Roe, Yuzu Emulsion
- Double Lamb Chop and Braised Shoulder with Argan Oil
- Chinese Braised Short Rib, Cucumber Yogurt, Thai Candied Mango

Desserts

- Buttermilk Panna Cotta, Olive Oil Cake, Blueberries, Anise Hyssop
- Chocolate Tart with Crispy Cherries
- Peach Salad with Mascarpone, Rhubarb, Meyer Lemon

Ferraro's

E2

Italian 🍴🍴

5900 W. Flamingo Rd. (bet Decatur & Jones Blvds.)

Phone: 702-364-5300
Web: www.ferraroslasvegas.com
Prices: $$

Mon – Fri lunch & dinner
Sat – Sun dinner only

Run by the Ferraro family since 1985, this elegant eatery exhibits true Italian warmth—especially for those seeking a departure from the huge, boisterous dining scene found in many hotels. Located less than three miles west of the Strip, where most restaurants are found in malls, Ferraro's benefits from being situated in a contemporary, European-style house bordering Flamingo Road.

Mimmo Ferraro (son of founder, Gino) heads the kitchen while maintaining the family's commitment to tradition. His menu focuses on classic dishes featuring house-made pasta, the signature osso buco, and Italian *dolci* such as tiramisu. In addition to the award-winning wine list, choose from a wide range of single-malt scotch, port, grappa, and cognac.

Most of the diners here are regulars, who are drawn back time after time by the polite, attentive staff, pleasant ambience, and serious cooking.

Gaylord India (Rio)

Indian ✗✗

A3

3700 W. Flamingo Rd.

Phone: 702-777-7923
Web: www.playrio.com
Prices: $$

Lunch & dinner daily

Sibling to the San Francisco stalwart of more than 30 years, Gaylord now makes another home in the Rio hotel, where its restful tone feels worlds away from the Vegas action. Beyond the two carved-wood elephants flanking the entrance, jewel-tone fabrics, Indian artifacts, and well-spaced, elegant tables tended by young, professional staff provide the background for fragrant Indian fare.

The expansive menu showcases fresh, subtly spiced Northern Indian cuisine, encompassing numerous meatless dishes as well as fixed-price options. For an authentic treat, select a combination menu featuring tandoori, curry, or lamb specialties accompanied by crisp samosas, traditional naan breads, a frothy *lassi* yogurt drink served salty or sweet, and Darjeeling tea.

The Champagne brunch is a popular option on Friday, Saturday, and Sunday.

J.C. Wooloughan (JW Marriott Resort)

D1

Gastropub ✗

221 N. Rampart Blvd. (at Summerlin Pkwy.)

Phone: 702-869-7725   Lunch & dinner daily
Web: www.jwlasvegasresort.com
Prices: ⊜⊜

A visit to this oh-so-Irish pub in the JW Marriott Resort *(see hotel listing)* is like taking a trip to the Emerald Isle. In fact, the entire place was designed and built outside Dublin, then taken apart, shipped across the Pond and reassembled in Las Vegas.

True to form, Wooloughan's menu includes a good selection of Irish whiskey and ale, but the real attraction here is the generous portions of pub food. Order up a pint while you ponder the menu; shepherd's pie crowned with a thick layer of "champ" (mashed potatoes) makes a hearty meal; but bangers 'n' mash or crispy fish 'n' chips (cod dipped in the house ale batter) are also tempting and authentic treats.

Finish up with the dense and delicious, syrup-saturated cake known as sticky toffee pudding, and you'll find yourself nostalgic for the Old Sod—whether or not you're Irish.

Marché Bacchus

French 🍴

D1

2620 Regatta Dr. (bet. Breakwater & Mariner Drs.)

Phone: 702-804-8008
Web: www.marchebacchus.com
Prices: $$$

Mon – Sat lunch & dinner
Sun lunch only

The god of wine himself would be happy to frequent this Summerlin wine shop, where more than 900 labels reveal an oenophile's atlas of the world's major growing regions. Of course, Bacchus would drop into the adjoining French bistro that bears his name to sate his hunger with a plate of traditional charcuterie or cheeses as a prelude to a hearty beef Bourgignon or comforting *poulet* frites. A rich *mousse au chocolat*, or a thin crust of puff pastry smeared with frangipane and topped with a fan of sliced apples might deliver the just desserts.

The Marché's new owners have extensively expanded the bistro's lovely lakeside patio, creating several levels of umbrella-shaded tables separated by steps, waterfalls, and bridges. No wonder that tables out here are highly coveted on a mild, sunny day.

Stop by on Saturdays for the free wine tastings.

Marché Bacchus

Marc's

Italian ✗✗

D1

7290 W. Lake Mead Blvd. (at Tenaya Way)

Phone:	702-562-1921	Mon – Fri lunch & dinner
Web:	www.marcsrestaurant.com	Sat – Sun dinner only
Prices:	**$$**	

The corner of a modern shopping strip marks the spot of this casual, neighborhood Italian restaurant. In the dining room, black linens cover the tables and booths line two side walls; outside, a patio faces the parking lot.

It's the generous servings of simple home-style Italian fare, not the décor, that keep locals coming back for more. Billing itself as an "Italian steakhouse," Marc's features a selection of prime steaks and Provimi veal. But tradition wouldn't be honored without the likes of eggplant parmesan, *pasta fagiola*, and wood-oven-roasted pizzas spread with velvety tomato sauce and finished off with such toppings as wild mushrooms or grilled basil chicken. References to the Rat Pack pepper the menu in Penne alla Dean Martin and Chicken Sinatra.

A more spirited menu touts a selection of martinis, perhaps another Rat Pack holdover.

Matt Meredith

West of The Strip

N9NE (Palms)

Steakhouse ✗✗✗

A3

4321 W. Flamingo Rd.

Dinner daily

Phone: 702-933-9900
Web: www.n9negroup.com
Prices: $$$$

With a hip vibe that would rival any in South Beach, N9NE burst upon the Vegas scene when the Palms resort *(see hotel listing)* opened in 2001. Chic chocolate suede booths and glittering columns that reflect the room's changing colored lights raise the stakes in this restaurant-cum-nightclub, frequented by as glamorous a crowd as you'll find anywhere in town.

Whether you go to see or be seen, don't miss out on the main attraction: prime aged steaks and chops. Perfectly seared and full of flavor, the meat is excellent by itself, or paired with Alaskan King crab legs or a Maine lobster tail and white-truffle aïoli as surf and turf.

This hot spot is part of the N9NE Group, founded in Chicago by Scott de Graff and Michael Morton. As the son of Arnie Morton—who founded the eponymous Chicago steakhouse chain—the latter partner comes by his calling naturally.

Nora's Cuisine

E2

Italian ✗

6020 W. Flamingo Rd. (at Jones Blvd.)

Phone:	702-365-6713
Web:	www.norascuisine.com
Prices:	💰💰

Mon – Fri lunch & dinner
Sat dinner only

This modest strip-mall neighborhood restaurant is well known to Vegas insiders. Founded by Nora and Gino Mauro in 1991, Nora's still cooks Italian comfort food with Sicilian accents. Here, the tone is unpretentious and service is speedy in casual dining rooms perpetually packed with casual crowds of regulars who would prefer to keep this place to themselves.

A display kitchen by the entrance features the brick oven, serving pizzas and grilled panini at bargain prices throughout the day. Dinnertime also delivers value, with *abbondonza*-sized servings of fresh gnocchi, pork tenderloin *alla Siciliana*, and much, much more on their expansive menu. All is done with an eye on tradition, comfort, and quality.

From a humble seating capacity of 12 when first opened, Nora's has mushroomed to accommodate 300 diners. A sports bar hosts live music on weekends.

Nove Italiano (Palms)

Italian ✕✕

A3

4321 W. Flamingo Rd.

Dinner daily

Phone: 702-942-6800
Web: www.n9negroup.com
Prices: $$$

Picture a roomful of glamorous diners who dress to impress, booming club music with surprisingly attentive service in an airy room that boasts stunning views of the Strip, and you see Nove. Italian for "nine," Nove makes a fitting moniker for the N9NE Group's sexy restaurant (sister to N9NE Steakhouse).

Travertine marble and Swarovski crystal bejewel the upscale dining room, while the seductive lounge is extended by breezy terraces and a mezzanine. Less extravagant than the décor, Chef Geno Bernardo's menu nonetheless holds its own with well-executed northern and southern Italian fare, completed by an A-list of varietals hailing from all the major wine-making regions of Italy.

A selection of fresh, well-prepared *crudo* begins the meal, which may progress through Italian variations on sashimi, pasta with meatballs and "Sunday gravy," or prime steaks.

N9NE Group

Ping Pang Pong (Gold Coast)

Chinese

4000 W. Flamingo Rd.
Phone: 702-247-8136
Web: www.goldcoastcasino.com
Prices:

Lunch & dinner daily

A local favorite, Ping Pang Pong hides inside the unpretentious Gold Coast casino, where it couches guests in one of two round rooms festooned with bright Japanese lanterns that cluster in the middle of the recessed ceiling.

The large exhibition kitchen dishes up acclaimed Chinese cuisine at low prices. As diverse as the many provinces of China that it spotlights, the menu wanders from clay pot rice and *congee* (porridge) past Emperor's seafood stew, Gobo beef, Majong noodles to the aromatic tea-smoked duck. "Provincial Favorites" include Cantonese pulled chicken tossed in five-spice dressing, and Dragon Well shrimp infused with green tea.

At lunchtime, Las Vegans crowd the place for dim sum. During this lively feast, waitresses make their rounds past each table bearing trays of aromatic savory and sweet little bites that may be steamed, crisp-fried, seared, or baked.

The Gold Coast Hotel and Casino

Rosemary's

American 🍴🍴

D2

8125 W. Sahara Ave. (bet. Buffalo Dr. & Cimarron Rd.)

Phone: 702-869-2251
Web: www.rosemarysrestaurant.com
Prices: $$

Mon – Fri lunch & dinner
Sat – Sun dinner only

A great neighborhood restaurant with a loyal following, Rosemary's continues to showcase skillfully prepared regional American dishes. Domestic products such as Maytag blue cheese, Anson Mills grits, and house-made steak sauce spark the menu with bold flavors. Songs of the South ring out in sides likes hoppin' John and hushpuppies—a tribute to Chef Michael Jordan's experience in New Orleans' kitchens.

Opened in 1999, Rosemary's consistently ranks as one of the top restaurants off the Strip. The crowds who come to this shopping center in search of fine cuisine in a low-key family ambience don't often leave disappointed. Locals in the know go for the three-course prix-fixe lunch—which offers a lot of bang for 28 bucks—or a similar menu, priced at $50, for dinner.

On Sunday night, Rosemary's offers half-price bottles of wine. Where on the Strip can you find a deal like that?

Rub (Rio)

Barbecue 🍴

3700 W. Flamingo Rd.

Phone: 702-227-0779
Web: www.rubbbq.net
Prices: $$

Mon – Thu dinner only
Fri – Sun lunch & dinner

Vegas brims with pit bosses, and now they have a pit master—barbecue pit, that is—at the Rio. A rub, in barbecue parlance, is a blend of dry spices used to coat the meat's exterior, as opposed to a wet sauce. In this case, though, the restaurant's name stands for "Righteous Urban Barbecue," a concept that Paul Kirk—aka the "Baron of Barbecue"—started in New York City.

At Rub, Chef Skip Steele, a Memphis boy who came to Vegas via St. Louis, proves his barbecue pedigree by slow-cooking St. Louis-style spare ribs, baby backs, sausages, and pastrami over wood for up to 14 hours. Specialties include burnt ends (the fattier point of the brisket), and Sichuan smoked ducks. If you show up with a group in tow, a platter called The Baron will feed folks deliciously with a smorgasbord-type tasting.

For a quirky Southern-inspired dessert, you just can't beat the deep-fried Oreos.

RUB BBQ

Sen of Japan

Japanese 🍴

D2

8480 W. Desert Inn Rd. (at Durango Dr.)

Phone: 702-871-7781

Web: www.senofjapan.com

Prices: $$

Dinner daily

Migrating from east of the Strip to west, Chef Hiro Nakano left Nobu at the Hard Rock Hotel to start his own place. The concept? Strip-quality sushi at off-Strip prices, and this place delivers. Expect supremely fresh fish in the form of traditional nigiri and new age maki.

If you go for the à la carte menu as opposed to the chef's omakase, your options are many. Begin, perhaps, with Shin's Special Nigiri Sushi Plate: seven different types of fish finished with different sauces and garnishes. Then, maybe, soy- and mirin-glazed black cod in lettuce cups—an unrepentant copy of a classic Nobu dish with a creative touch. Nightly special maki run to inspired combinations such as sweet shrimp, crispy shrimp tempura, mango, and pungent red onion.

Add a local clientele, a casual vibe combined with friendly service, late hours, and a large parking lot—and who could ask for more?

Sen of Japan

Shizen (JW Marriott Resort)

D1

J a p a n e s e

221 N. Rampart Blvd. (at Summerlin Pkwy.)
Phone: 702-869-7900   Dinner daily
Web: www.jwlasvegasresort.com
Prices: $$

Both resort guests and Summerlin residents favor the extensive sushi selection at Shizen, located at the lush JW Marriott Las Vegas Resort *(see hotel listing).* In addition to the reasonably priced nigiri and sashimi served at the expansive bar, innovative specialty rolls encompass choices from the Tempura Crunch of shrimp, crab, *gobo, takuwan,* cucumber, avocado, and *masago;* to the Las Vegas, showcasing buttery tuna, yellowtail, and salmon.

Those who enjoy a show during dinner should head for one of the teppanyaki tables, where chefs prepare enticing combinations of meat, fish, and vegetables on large flat-top grills before eager diners. Those seeking more traditional seating may prefer to order à la carte in the large dining room.

Shizen makes a particularly good alternative for Japanese food west of the Strip, since the fresh food here can be enjoyed for off-Strip prices.

Terra Rossa (Red Rock Resort)

D2

11011 W. Charleston Blvd. (at I-215)

Lunch & dinner daily

Phone: 702-797-7576
Web: www.redrocklasvegas.com
Prices: $$

Terra Rossa resides inside the Red Rock Resort *(see hotel listing)*, which is named for the stunning Red Rock Canyon National Conservation Area that surrounds it.

Quality, skill, and freshness may trump innovation, but this only enhances enjoyment for those who crave traditional Italian fare. Top-notch ingredients and classic Mediterranean flavors ring true in entrées such as almond-crusted tuna *Siciliana* with orange raisin sauce; or chicken *al mattone*, grilled under a brick. The modern, elegant dining area offers a partial view of the kitchen turning out well-prepared antipasti, pizza, and pasta dishes in generous portions.

Friendly and attentive service in this casual-chic atmosphere make Terra Rossa popular with both hotel guests and locals. Although the main dining room is often packed, a full menu is available at the backlit marble bar.

West of The Strip

165

Thai Spice

Thai ✕

A3

4433 W. Flamingo Rd. (at Arville St.)

Phone: 702-362-5308
Web: N/A
Prices: 💿

Mon – Sat lunch & dinner

Thai Spice may be lackluster in décor, showcasing a few Asian artifacts, framed photographs, and perhaps a bouquet of flowers, but this unassuming strip-mall find is striking in terms of its cuisine. The restaurant consistently wins local raves for its extensive offerings of authentic and inexpensive Thai dishes. These may include spicy *Pa-Nang* beef simmered in red curry and coconut cream; a good selection of seasoned salads; as well as mint leaf chicken with chiles. Be sure to tell the waiter your preferred level of heat, being forewarned that "medium spicy" results in a tongue-tingling Thai interpretation. A list of pleasing desserts features the likes of mellow and sweet coconut custard.

Look for Thai Spice in a little shopping center a block away from The Palms Hotel and easily accessible from the Strip—where food this good cannot be found for prices this low.

Vintner Grill

Mediterranean ✗✗

D1

10100 W. Charleston Blvd. (bet. Hualapai Way & Indigo Dr.)

Lunch & dinner daily

Phone: 702-214-5590
Web: www.vglasvegas.com
Prices: $$

Chic, sophisticated, and flaunting an elegant contemporary style that upgrades its office-plaza location, Vintner Grill lures ladies-who-lunch in the wealthy Vegas suburb of Summerlin. The décor is a study in cool green and white, complete with a wine room and a tall communal table with a view of the exhibition kitchen.

Skillful hands turn first-rate ingredients into Mediterranean dishes that dress to impress. The menu changes daily, but a pan-seared crab cake sparked by garlic aïoli; wood-fired flatbreads; and lamb osso buco with toasted barley risotto hint at what you might find. Desserts such as a caramelized lemon-curd tart served with boysenberry sauce and a scoop of pistachio ice cream may prove too tempting to resist.

Outside, white cabanas punctuate the romantic tree-shaded patio, lit by flickering candles and metal lanterns strung through the trees.

Viva Mercado's

Mexican ✗

3553 S. Rainbow Blvd. (at Spring Mountain Rd.)

Phone: 702-871-8826 Lunch & dinner daily
Web: www.vivamercadoslv.com
Prices: ⬮⬮

After years at a much smaller strip-mall setting, Viva Mercado's has moved to a spacious stand-alone building on Rainbow Boulevard with an ample parking lot. Owner Bobby Mercado's new space boasts several different dining rooms, the largest of which can seat 225 people.

It's a casual scene here, catering to a business crowd at lunch and families at dinner. All appreciate the large portions of tasty Mexican food, made with fresh ingredients. Lunch begins with a basket of multicolored tortilla chips and little bowls of pinto bean purée, and smoky red-chile salsa for dipping. A good bargain if you're watching your wallet, combinations feature all the usual suspects: tacos, tamales, burritos, and enchiladas.

At dinner there's a wide range of entrées, in addition to a choice of salsas from a list that's rated according to the degree of heat (the habañero is the hottest).

Downtown

Although the "other" Las Vegas often gets overlooked in favor of the famed Strip of Las Vegas Boulevard, Downtown is where the seeds of glitz and glamour that now define the city first sprouted.

Let There Be Light— Neon, That Is

When the humble railroad post of Las Vegas was incorporated as a city in March 1911, the Downtown spine of Fremont Street was an unlikely party center, due to the fact that bars were forbidden along its length. The thoroughfare livened up as would-be bar owners figured out they could get liquor licenses by opening hotels—often with very few rooms. Legalized gambling juiced things up further in 1931, when The Northern Club was granted the first Nevada gaming license. By the 40s, casino-lined Fremont Street shined as a neon "Glitter Gulch." But it was not until 1946—the same year that the iconic 48-foot-tall neon cowboy unofficially named Vegas Vic rose over the Pioneer Club—that the Golden Nugget become Fremont's first building constructed as a casino.

All That Glitters

Vic's still there, but the Nugget's original sign lies in the Neon Museum—a casualty of Steve Wynn's 1980s-era renovation. Wynn started the Strip's mega-resort renaissance as civic leaders in the 90s pondered how to keep Glitter Gulch aglow. The **Fremont Street Experience**, a nightly light (some 16 million) and sound extravaganza, was the answer. The five-block pedestrian zone now boasts 10 casinos, more than 60 restaurants, and too many bars to count. Third Street, particularly, is a hotspot for trendy bistros and bars.

Downtown's serious side centers on a booming business and government center. In 2005, the Las Vegas Market opened as a state-of-the-art exhibit space for the retail furniture and design trade. Plans continue for the 12-million-square-foot World Market Center, which will encompass exhibit space in 8 buildings on 57 contiguous acres downtown. When completed in 2012, the center will combine all segments of the industry on one mega-campus. Also in the works is the 61-acre Union Park development with proposed medical and performing-arts centers, high rises, and the World Jewelry Center. The Arts Factory on Charleston Boulevard now anchors a thriving Arts District. Flashiest of all, perhaps, is still Vegas Vic, whose friendly figure welcomes visitors to Las Vegas as it has for six decades.

Downtown

© Mark Gibson

Andre's ✿

Downtown

A6

French 🍴🍴

401 S. 6th St. (bet. Bridger & Clark Aves.)

Tue – Sat dinner only

Phone: 702-385-5016
Web: www.andrelv.com
Prices: $$$$

For a traditional French meal, there is no better choice in town than this timeless auberge, which evokes a Gallic farmhouse with its rough stucco walls, beamed ceilings, and walls decorated with colorful crockery.

Long before Las Vegas claimed a constellation of star chefs, Andre's reigned as the city's special-occasion restaurant. And so it is today, for those who feel nostalgic for the time when folks favored French cuisine *sans* any fear of cholesterol and calories. Thus, you will savor lavish old-world dishes such as tender medallions of rabbit loin stuffed with sweet crab meat; and an oven-roasted poussin served over a thick jus studded with porcini mushrooms, spring peas, and bits of foie gras.

An extensive list of French and California wines pairs with Chef/owner André Rochat's private collection of Cognac and Armagnac— which is displayed in the front reception and bar areas.

Appetizers	*Entrées*	*Desserts*
• Pan-seared Foie Gras, Thai Spice Crust, French Toast	• Dover Sole Véronique, Grenobloise or Amandine, with Potato Rissole, Spring Vegetables	• Warm Apple Tarte Tatin, Calvados Ice Cream and Caramel Sauce
• Smoked Salmon-wrapped Scallops, Celery Fondant	• King Crab-stuffed Rabbit Loin, Mushroom Gnocchi, Tomato, Natural Jus	• "Extase Soufflé"
• Jambon de Bayonne, Caponata "Agrodolce"		• André's Caramelized Lemon Tart with Seasonal Berries

Casa Don Juan

Mexican

A6

1204 S. Main St. (at California St.)

Phone: 702-384-8070

Web: N/A

Prices:

Lunch & dinner daily

In downtown Las Vegas, where good food can be hard to find, casual Casa Don Juan ranks as a hacienda apart for its bright, cheerful décor and good, simple Mexican food. In the main dining room, mirrors reflect light throughout the space; while yellow walls, orange tiles, and vivid portraits of Mexican artist Frida Kahlo add to the ambience. There's a second room, to the right of the entrance, where guests can watch the tortilla maker rolling out the flour and corn dough that form the base for many of the dishes, including the chicken and cheese enchiladas that come liberally doused with a mildly spicy red chile sauce. Bounteous portions and low prices keep patrons coming back.

A local watering hole, Don Juan welcomes families as well as downtown business people with friendly and efficient service from waitresses clad in colorful flounced skirts and white blouses.

Grotto (Golden Nugget)

A5

Italian ✕

129 E. Fremont St. (at 1st St.)

Phone: 702-386-8341

Web: www.grottorestaurants.com

Prices: $$

Lunch & dinner daily

As the first luxury hotel to open in Las Vegas (1946), the Golden Nugget *(see hotel listing)* has undergone a lot of changes over the years. The most recent renovations, made in 2006, included the addition of Grotto Ristorante.

A casual Italian trattoria, Grotto is located just past the lobby reception area, where it sits slightly raised above the casino floor. Here, diners enjoy a view of the $30-million pool, which includes a 200,000-gallon shark tank. If memories of *Jaws* make you squeamish, turn your attention to the exhibition pizza oven and antipasti station, where you can watch chefs prepare something for you to eat, instead of watching something that might fancy eating you.

Prompt, cordial service, and heaping plates of homemade pastas, thin-crust pizzas, and meat and fish entrées make this roomy restaurant a winner with families, groups and hotel guests alike.

Courtesy of The Golden Nugget

Vic & Anthony's (Golden Nugget)

Steakhouse ✗✗✗

A5

129 E. Fremont St. (at 1st St.)

Phone: 702-386-8399   Dinner daily
Web: www.vicandanthonys.com
Prices: $$$

Downtown Las Vegas is steakhouse central, where every hotel seems to claim a restaurant honoring meat in its many forms. Vic & Anthony's fits the mold with its dark, clubby atmosphere, full of wood paneling, leather chairs and candlelight.

Your satisfaction is the staff's command here. When servers bring your steak to the table, they will request that you cut into it to make sure that the meat is cooked to your liking. Who wouldn't like a juicy filet mignon, perfectly seared until the outside is crisp and the inside is tender and moist? Or an appetizer of maple-glazed quail, sticky-sweet and deep brown, and drizzled with spicy Sriracha sauce made from ground chile, garlic and vinegar? Of course, lobster and a few other seafood choices make their required appearance.

Dining alone? Don't let all the couples intimidate you; the full menu is available at the bar.

Courtesy of the Golden Nugget

175

Where to **stay**

© Tim Pannell/Corbis

Alphabetical list of Hotels

Where to stay

Bellagio

3600 Las Vegas Blvd. S. (at Flamingo Rd.)

Phone: 702-693-7111 or 888-987-3456
Fax: 702-693-8555
Web: www.bellagio.com
Prices: $$$

3421
Rooms
512
Suites

Inspired by the Italian village of Bellagio on the shores of Lake Como, Steve Wynn's *bellisimo* resort changed the face of the Strip in 1998. Wynn sunk a whopping $1.6 billion into his gargantuan hotel (now owned by MGM Mirage group), which fronts an 8-acre lake famed for its fountain and light shows.

Dale Chihuly's breathtaking sculpture *Fiori di Como* blooms across the lobby ceiling in a rainbow of hand-blown glass flowers. The real flora, however, bursts into view in the nearby Conservatory, where a stunning array of flora changes with the season.

Guests can choose their accommodations among 3,933 spacious rooms and 512 suites. The seven suite types recently underwent a $60 million redesign; warm mahogany wood, cool marble, and sumptuous fabrics now raise the bar on in-suite luxury.

In addition to the fabulous spa, the Cirque de Soleil water show "O," a fine-art gallery, and a wealth of restaurants, Bellagio boasts a new nightspot—The Bank—that centers on a glass-encased dance floor.

The Strip

Where to eat...

The Strip

Bellagio

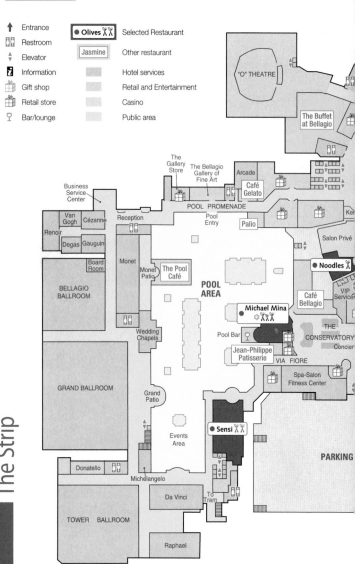

Legend:

- ↑ Entrance
- 🚻 Restroom
- ↕ Elevator
- ℹ Information
- 🎁 Gift shop
- 🏬 Retail store
- ♀ Bar/lounge

- ● Olives ✕ — Selected Restaurant
- Jasmine — Other restaurant
- Hotel services
- Retail and Entertainment
- Casino
- Public area

Map labels:

"O" THEATRE

The Buffet at Bellagio

The Gallery Store

The Bellagio Gallery of Fine Art

Arcade

Café Gelato

Business Service Center

Van Gogh

Cézanne

Renoir

Reception

POOL PROMENADE

Pool Entry

Palio

Ken

Degas

Gauguin

Salon Privé

Board Room

Monet

Monet Patio

The Pool Café

POOL AREA

● Noodles ✕

Café Bellagio

VIP Service

BELLAGIO BALLROOM

● Michael Mina ✕✕✕

THE CONSERVATORY

Concier

Wedding Chapels

Pool Bar ♀

Jean-Philippe Patisserie

VIA FIORE

GRAND BALLROOM

Spa-Salon Fitness Center

Grand Patio

Events Area

● Sensi ✕✕

PARKING

Donatello

Michelangelo

To Tram

TOWER BALLROOM

Da Vinci

Raphael

The Strip

180

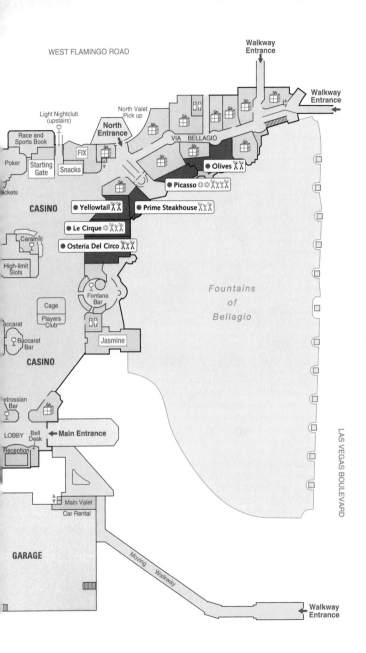

WEST FLAMINGO ROAD

Walkway Entrance

Walkway Entrance

Light Nightclub (upstairs)

North Valet Pick up

North Entrance

VIA BELLAGIO

Race and Sports Book

FIX

Snacks

Poker

Starting Gate

Olives

● Picasso ❋❋

● Yellowtail

● Prime Steakhouse

CASINO

● Le Cirque ❋

Caramel

● Osteria Del Circo

High-limit Slots

Fontana Bar

Fountains of Bellagio

Cage

Players Club

Baccarat

Jasmine

Baccarat Bar

CASINO

Petrossian Bar

Main Entrance

LOBBY

Bell Desk

Reception

Main Valet

Car Rental

GARAGE

Moving Walkway

Walkway Entrance

LAS VEGAS BOULEVARD

Caesars Palace

 B3

3570 Las Vegas Blvd S. (at Flamingo Rd.)

Phone: 702-731-7110 or 866-227-5938
Fax: 702-967-3890
Web: www.caesarspalace.com
Prices: $$$

1834
Rooms
1504
Suites

Friends, Romans, Countrymen … there will soon be room for everyone in this Greco-Roman extravaganza, which is in the process of a billion-dollar expansion (to open in 2009).

The expansion's centerpiece will be the new 23-story Octavius Tower that will add 665 rooms to the property's present count of 3,340. Set on 85 acres in the middle of the Strip, Caesars Palace reigns over 24 restaurants, 5 nightclubs, 5 wedding chapels, 3 heated, outdoor swimming pools, 3 casinos, 24,000 square feet of meeting space, acres of designer shops, and a 4,300-seat Colosseum that books headliners like Bette Midler and Cher.

Julius Caesar himself would have felt at home at the Vegas palace that bears his name, amid the immense fountains, statues, and soaring marble columns that define the classical architecture inside and out. It's likely the emperor would prefer the luxury of the Augustus Tower rooms, appointed with a fax machine, flat-screen TVs, and marble baths with oversized spa tubs.

All hail, Caesars.

The Strip

Where to eat...

The Strip

Caesars Palace

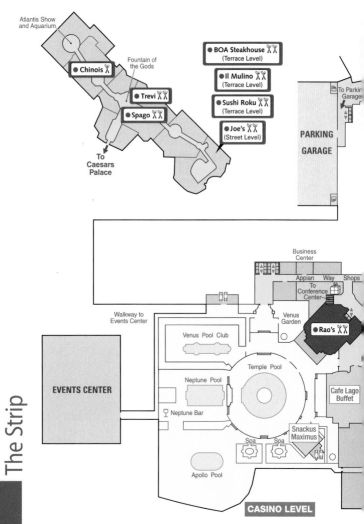

Atlantis Show
and Aquarium

Fountain of
the Gods

● Chinois X

● Trevi XX

● Spago XX

To
Caesars
Palace

● BOA Steakhouse XX
(Terrace Level)

● Il Mulino XX
(Terrace Level)

● Sushi Roku XX
(Terrace Level)

● Joe's XX
(Street Level)

To Parking
Garage

**PARKING
GARAGE**

Business
Center

Appian   Way   Shops
To
Conference
Center

Venus
Garden

Walkway to
Events Center

Venus Pool Club

● Rao's XX

Temple Pool

EVENTS CENTER

Neptune Pool

♀ Neptune Bar

Spa   Spa

Apollo Pool

Snackus
Maximus

Cafe Lago
Buffet

CASINO LEVEL

The Strip

184

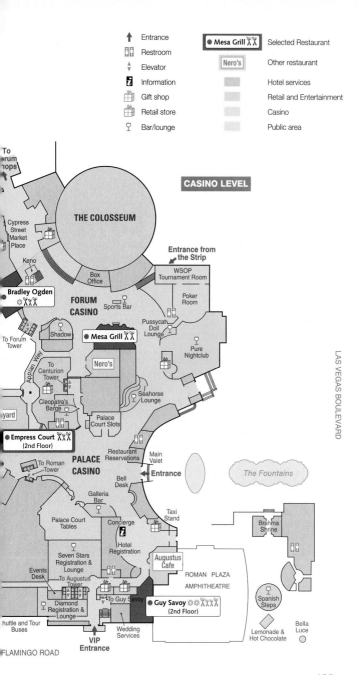

Legend

- ↑ Entrance
- Restroom
- ↕ Elevator
- Information
- Gift shop
- Retail store
- Bar/lounge

- ● **Mesa Grill** Selected Restaurant
- Nero's Other restaurant
- Hotel services
- Retail and Entertainment
- Casino
- Public area

CASINO LEVEL

To Forum Shops

Cypress Street Market Place

Keno

THE COLOSSEUM

Bradley Ogden

Box Office

Entrance from the Strip

WSOP Tournament Room

Poker Room

FORUM CASINO

Sports Bar

Shadow

● **Mesa Grill**

Pussycat Doll Lounge

Pure Nightclub

To Forum Tower

Appian Way

To Centurion Tower

Nero's

Cleopatra's Barge

Seahorse Lounge

...yard

Palace Court Slots

● **Empress Court** (2nd Floor)

Restaurant Reservations

Main Valet

PALACE CASINO

To Roman Tower

Bell Desk

Entrance

Galleria Bar

Palace Court Tables

Taxi Stand

The Fountains

Brahma Shrine

Concierge

Seven Stars Registration & Lounge

Hotel Registration

Augustus Cafe

ROMAN PLAZA AMPHITHEATRE

Events Desk

To Augustus Tower

Diamond Registration & Lounge

To Guy Savoy

● **Guy Savoy** (2nd Floor)

Spanish Steps

Shuttle and Tour Buses

Wedding Services

Lemonade & Hot Chocolate

Bella Luce

VIP Entrance

FLAMINGO ROAD

LAS VEGAS BOULEVARD

Mandalay Bay

3950 Las Vegas Blvd. S. (at Mandalay Bay Rd.)

Phone: 702-632-7777 or 877-632-7000
Fax: 702-891-7270
Web: www.mandalaybay.com
Prices: $$$

2775
Rooms
436
Suites

Spa

Life's a beach at Mandalay Bay. At the south end of the Strip, this tropical fantasy encompasses an 11-acre beach, complete with waves and 2,700 tons of real sand. And while sand is in no short supply around these desert parts, the breakers *are* unique. A recent $30-million beach expansion added a three-story, climate-controlled Beachside Casino, offering everything from beachfront blackjack to über-luxurious private villas available for day use.

With more than 4,700 rooms between the original hotel and connecting properties THEhotel and The Four Seasons, you can take your pick of motifs. The original resort retains its South Seas theme with the awesome Shark Reef, where you'll be surrounded (in glass tunnels) by 15 types of sharks. Next door, the 43-story tower called THEhotel caters to the young and the hip with bold, contemporary décor and spacious well-equipped suites. Known for impeccable service, The Four Seasons occupies floors 35 to 39 of Mandalay Bay, lending elegance to the mix.

The Strip

MGM Mirage

Where to eat…

▶ *RECOMMENDED*

Aureole ✿	✗✗✗	33
Border Grill	✗✗	37
Charlie Palmer Steak	✗✗✗	42
China Grill	✗✗	43
Fleur de Lys	✗✗✗	59
miX ✿	✗✗✗	71
The Noodle Shop	✗	77
rm seafood	✗✗✗	90
rumjungle	✗✗	91
Stripsteak	✗✗	102
Trattoria del Lupo	✗✗	110
Verandah	✗✗✗	113

▶ *ALSO*

House of Blues
Red Square
Red, White & Blue
Shanghai Lilly

The Strip

Mandalay Bay

HACIENDA AVENUE

Registration

VIP lounge

the lounge

the coffee bar

MANDALAY BAY THEATRE

THEhotel at Mandalay Bay

the café

● miX ☼ 🍴🍴🍴 (64th Floor)

● rumjungle 🍴🍴

THEhotel Entrance and Valet

Ra and Sp Bo

Red Squa

PARKING GARAGE

● Trattoria del Lupo 🍴🍴

● China Grill 🍴🍴

● Stripsteak 🍴🍴

Red, White and Bl

FRANK SINATRA BOULEVARD

Starbucks

Shangh Lilly

Box Office

EVENTS CENTER (CONCOURSE LEVEL)

Satellite Race and Sports Book

Event Center Bar

VIP ticketing

NORTH CONVENTION CENTER

● Border Grill 🍴

The Strip

Convention Center Main Entrance

SOUTH CONVENTION CENTER

Shark Reef a Mandalay Ba

Food Court

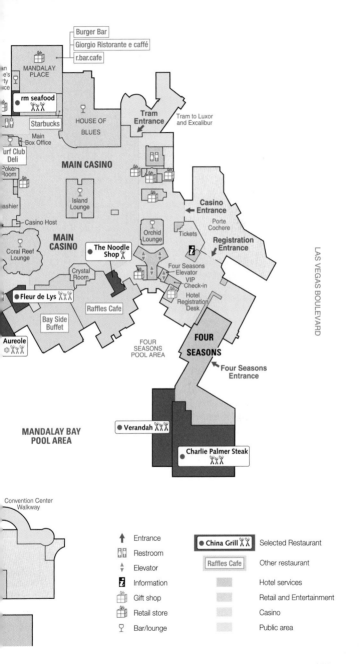

Burger Bar
Giorgio Ristorante e caffé
r.bar.cafe

MANDALAY PLACE

rm seafood

Starbucks

HOUSE OF BLUES

Tram Entrance

Tram to Luxor and Excalibur

Main Box Office

Turf Club Deli

Poker Room

MAIN CASINO

Island Lounge

Casino Entrance

Porte Cochere

Cashier

Casino Host

Orchid Lounge

Tickets

Registration Entrance

MAIN CASINO

The Noodle Shop

Coral Reef Lounge

Four Seasons Elevator

VIP Check-in

Crystal Room

Fleur de Lys

Raffles Cafe

Hotel Registration Desk

Bay Side Buffet

Aureole

FOUR SEASONS POOL AREA

FOUR SEASONS

Four Seasons Entrance

MANDALAY BAY POOL AREA

Verandah

Charlie Palmer Steak

LAS VEGAS BOULEVARD

Convention Center Walkway

↑ Entrance
⊞ Restroom
↕ Elevator
🛈 Information
🎁 Gift shop
🏬 Retail store
🍸 Bar/lounge

● China Grill Selected Restaurant
Raffles Cafe Other restaurant
Hotel services
Retail and Entertainment
Casino
Public area

MGM Grand

3799 Las Vegas Blvd. S. (at Tropicana Ave.)

Phone: 702-891-7777 or 877-880-0880
Fax: 702-891-3036
Web: www.mgmgrand.com
Prices: $$$

4293
Rooms
751
Suites

Guarded by a 100,000-pound bronze statue of the MGM lion, the MGM Grand roars with some of the best entertainment and dining in Vegas. The lineup includes The Hollywood Theatre, the pyrotechnics-sparked Cirque de Soleil show KÀ, and space for concerts and championship boxing in the 16,800-seat Grand Garden Arena. Set next to the hotel's conference center, the new Marquee Ballroom can host 6,000 guests in style. And if the names Joël Robuchon, Tom Colicchio, Michael Mina, and Wolfgang Puck make your mouth water, you're in luck; they all have restaurants here.

Deluxe rooms are well-appointed in Art Deco style and offer space to spread out in large closets, on work desks, and in sitting areas. King rooms in the West Wing are quiet (rollaway beds and cribs are not allowed in this wing) and ultra-modern in décor.

Kicking up the level of luxury, the Tony Chi-designed Skylofts boast private elevator access, stellar views, and 24-hour butler service, while Signature at MGM Grand gives guests a sumptuous residential option.

The Strip

Where to eat…

The Strip

MGM Grand

↑ Entrance

🚻 Restroom

↕ Elevator

ℹ Information

🎁 Gift shop

🛍 Retail store

Y Bar/lounge

● Emeril's 🍴   Selected Restaurant

Studio Café   Other restaurant

Hotel services

Retail and Entertainment

Casino

Public area

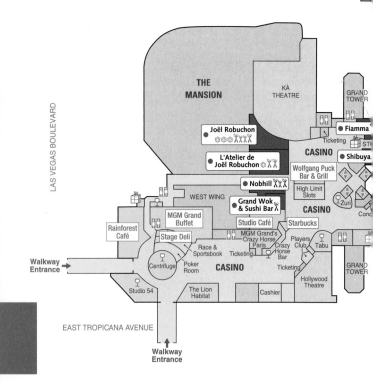

LAS VEGAS BOULEVARD

THE MANSION

KÀ THEATRE

GRAND TOWER

● Fiamma

Joël Robuchon 🍴🍴🍴

Ticketing

CASINO

● Shibuya

L'Atelier de Joël Robuchon 🍴

Wolfgang Puck Bar & Grill

● Nobhill 🍴🍴🍴

High Limit Slots

WEST WING

Grand Wok & Sushi Bar 🍴

Zuri

CASINO

Conc

Studio Café

Starbucks

MGM Grand Buffet

Rainforest Café

Stage Deli

MGM Grand's Crazy Horse Paris

Players Club

Tabu

Centrifuge

Race & Sportsbook

Crazy Horse Bar

GRAND TOWER

Poker Room

Ticketing

CASINO

Ticketing

Hollywood Theatre

Walkway Entrance →

Studio 54

The Lion Habitat

Cashier

EAST TROPICANA AVENUE

↑ Walkway Entrance

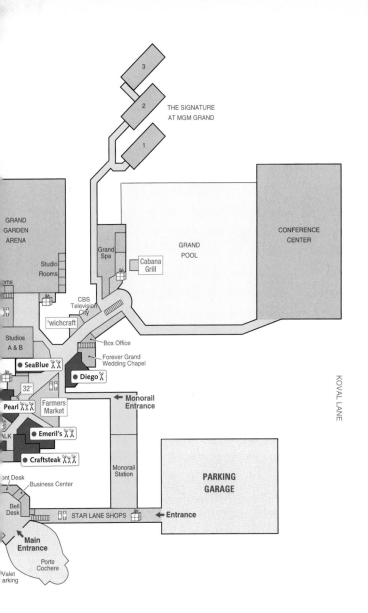

THE SIGNATURE
AT MGM GRAND

3

2

1

GRAND
GARDEN
ARENA

Studio
Rooms

oms

Grand
Spa

Cabana
Grill

GRAND
POOL

CONFERENCE
CENTER

CBS
Television
City

'wichcraft

Box Office

Studios
A & B

Forever Grand
Wedding Chapel

● SeaBlue ✕✕

● Diego ✕

32'

● Monorail
Entrance

Pearl ✕✕✕

Farmers
Market

ALK

● Emeril's ✕✕

● Craftsteak ✕✕✕

ont Desk

Business Center

Monorail
Station

PARKING
GARAGE

Bell
Desk

STAR LANE SHOPS

● Entrance

Main
Entrance

Porte
Cochere

Valet
arking

KOVAL LANE

EAST TROPICANA AVENUE

Mirage

 B3

3400 Las Vegas Blvd. S.
(bet. Flamingo Rd. & Spring Mountain Rd.)

Phone: 702-791-7111 or 800-627-6667
Fax: 702-791-7446
Web: www.mirage.com
Prices: $$

2763
Rooms
281
Suites

This Polynesian paradise opened in 1989, leading off the boom of themed megaresorts that popped up along the Strip in the 90s. She may look a bit less glamorous now, eclipsed by newest neighbors Palazzo, Wynn, and Encore, but this lady is no tramp.

A recent facelift has revamped the guest rooms in bold contemporary style. Promoting relaxation, rooms now flaunt pillow-top mattresses, 42-inch LCD TVs, and doors that close with a whisper instead of a bang.

Other new features include Chef Laurent Tourondel's casual BLT Burger (opened in spring 2008); a restoration of the hotel's signature volcano; and the newly designed spa and Kim Vo (the TV makeover guy) salon. The Royal White Tiger Habitat is permanently closed, but these magnificent cats still roam Siegfried and Roy's Secret Garden and Dolphin Habitat.

However some things haven't changed: the lush atrium rainforest still flourishes with towering palm trees, bright orchids, and cascading waterfalls.

The Strip

MGM Mirage

Where to eat...

▶ *RECOMMENDED*

▶ *ALSO*

The Strip

Mirage

CASINO LEVEL

Entrance	
Restroom	
Elevator	
Information	
Gift shop	
Retail store	
Bar/lounge	
● Fin — Selected Restaurant	
Samba — Other restaurant	
Hotel services	
Retail and Entertainment	
Casino	
Public area	

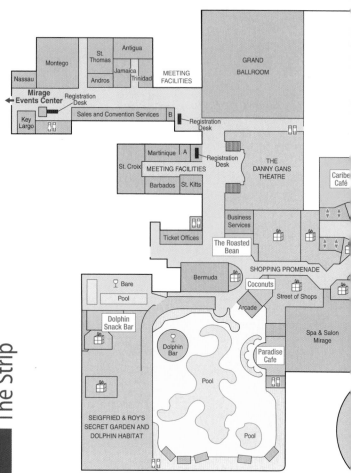

Montego
Nassau
St. Thomas
Antigua
Jamaica
Andros
Trinidad
MEETING FACILITIES
GRAND BALLROOM
Mirage Events Center
Registration Desk
Key Largo
Sales and Convention Services
B
Registration Desk
St. Croix
Martinique
A
Registration Desk
MEETING FACILITIES
Barbados
St. Kitts
THE DANNY GANS THEATRE
Caribe Café
Business Services
Ticket Offices
The Roasted Bean
SHOPPING PROMENADE
Bermuda
Coconuts
Street of Shops
Bare
Pool
Arcade
Dolphin Snack Bar
Dolphin Bar
Paradise Cafe
Spa & Salon Mirage
Pool
SEIGFRIED & ROY'S SECRET GARDEN AND DOLPHIN HABITAT
Pool

The Strip

196

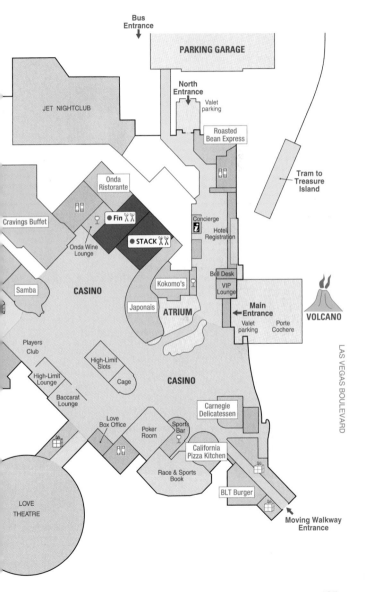

Bus Entrance

PARKING GARAGE

North Entrance

Valet parking

JET NIGHTCLUB

Roasted Bean Express

Tram to Treasure Island

Onda Ristorante

Concierge

Cravings Buffet

● Fin

Hotel Registration

Onda Wine Lounge

● STACK

Bell Desk

Samba

Kokomo's

VIP Lounge

Main Entrance

CASINO

Japonais

ATRIUM

VOLCANO

Valet parking

Porte Cochere

Players Club

High-Limit Slots

High-Limit Lounge

Cage

CASINO

LAS VEGAS BOULEVARD

Baccarat Lounge

Carnegie Delicatessen

Love Box Office

Poker Room

Sports Bar

California Pizza Kitchen

Race & Sports Book

BLT Burger

LOVE THEATRE

Moving Walkway Entrance

Palazzo

3325 Las Vegas Blvd. S. (at Sands Ave.)

Phone: 702-607-7777 or 877-883-6423
Fax: 866-263-3001
Web: www.palazzolasvegas.com
Prices: $$$$

3066
Suites

The Las Vegas skyline is constantly rising, and this $1.9 billion, 50-story luxury tower does more than measure up. Sheathed in some seven acres of glass and accented inside with 11,000 tons of marble, The Palazzo opened its doors in January 2008. It is owned by the same group that operates The Venetian, and connects to its Italian cousin through the Shoppes at Palazzo.

In every other way, however, the Palazzo is a separate resort. The refined hotel has its own entrance, its own Canyon Ranch Spa Club®, its own collection of top-chef restaurants, and its own show—Jersey Boys. All accommodations are suites, flaunting sunken living rooms with plenty of seating, and desks with high-speed Internet access and a fax/copier/printer. Featherbeds swathed in Egyptian linens will lull you to sleep; three flat-screen TVs ensure you won't miss a minute of your favorite show.

For fast-car aficionados, Palazzo rivals Wynn's Ferrari-Maserati dealership with its own Lamborghini showroom.

The Strip

The Palazzo

Where to eat...

▶ *RECOMMENDED*

▶ *ALSO*

Dos Caminos
LAVO
Mainland
Woo

The Strip

Palazzo

CASINO LEVEL

● Table 10 🍴🍴   Selected Restaurant

Dos Caminos   Other restaurant

↑   Entrance

🚻   Restroom

↕   Elevator

ℹ️   Information

🎁   Gift shop

🎁   Retail store

🍸   Bar/lounge

   Hotel services

   Retail and Entertainment

   Casino

   Public area

EAST SANDS AVENUE

Grand Lux Cafe

● SUSHISAMBA 🍴🍴
(Retail Level)

CASINO

Restaurant Charlie
❄️🍴🍴🍴

to
The Shoppes at
The Palazzo

● Table 10 🍴🍴
(Retail Level)

CASINO

to
Parking ↑

Pedestrian Bridge over
Spring Mountain Rd. ◄

High-Limit
Slots

🍸
VIP
Lounge

🚻

● Carnevino 🍴🍴

Front
desk

Concierge

● Morels 🍴🍴

LOBBY

Street Level
Entrance to ►
40/40 Club

The Strip

LAS VEGAS BOULEVARD

● Dal Toro 🍴
(Lower Level)

🎁 Lamborghini
(Lower Level)

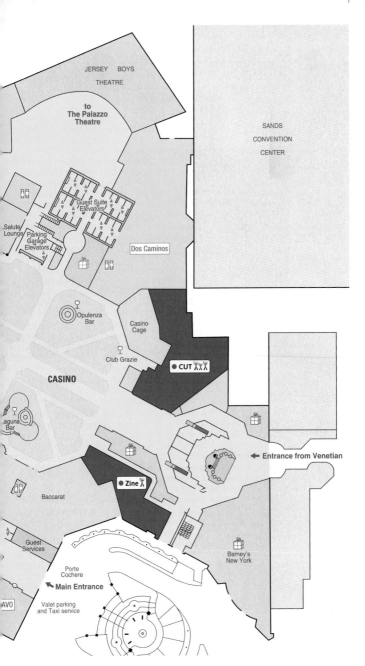

JERSEY BOYS
THEATRE

to
The Palazzo
Theatre

SANDS
CONVENTION
CENTER

Guest Suite
Elevators

Salute/
Lounge
Parking
Garage
Elevators

Dos Caminos

Opulenza
Bar

Casino
Cage

Club Grazie

● CUT

CASINO

Laguna
Bar

← Entrance from Venetian

● Zine

Baccarat

Guest
Services

Barney's
New York

Porte
Cochere

← Main Entrance

AVO

Valet parking
and Taxi service

Paris

3655 Las Vegas Blvd. S. (bet. Flamingo Rd. & Harmon Ave.)

Phone: 702-946-7000 or 877-796-2096
Fax: 702-946-4405
Web: www.parislasvegas.com
Prices: **$$**

2621
Rooms
295
Suites

French *joie de vivre* pervades this visually entertaining resort, beginning with the lobby, dripping with gilt trim and glittering crystal chandeliers. Faux-cobblestone pathways lead through the casino area, under a bright-blue "sky" ceiling painted with puffy white clouds.

Outside, the observation deck on the 50-story model of the *Tour Eiffel* may overlook the neon of the Strip, but when you see the Arc de Triomph and the façades of the Louvre, the Opéra, and the Hôtel de Ville below, you might believe you're in the real City of Light. (Original plans called for the Eiffel Tower to match the size of its twin in Paris, but air-traffic-control concerns at McCarran International Airport forced the architects to reduce the tower to half-scale.)

In the rooms, curves and cabriole legs define the custom European furnishings, fine linens cover the bed, and pink marble lines the bathroom. Paris connects to its sister property, Bally's, via Le Boulevard, a Parisian-style shopping "avenue."

The Strip

Where to eat...

▶ *Recommended*
Eiffel Tower	✗✗✗	53
Mon Ami Gabi	✗✗	72

▶ *Also*
Le Provençal
Les Artistes Steakhouse
Le Village Buffet

The Strip

Paris

CASINO LEVEL

↑ Entrance	● Eiffel Tower 🍴 Selected Restaurant
Restroom	Ah Sin — Other restaurant
Elevator	Hotel services
ℹ Information	Retail and Entertainment
Gift shop	Casino
Retail store	Public area
♀ Bar/lounge	

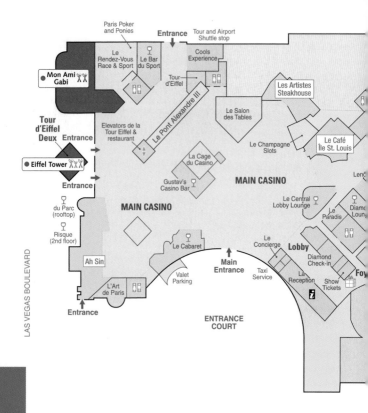

Paris Poker and Ponies
Entrance
Tour and Airport Shuttle stop
Le Rendez-Vous Race & Sport
Le Bar du Sport
Cools Experience
● Mon Ami Gabi 🍴
Tour d'Eiffel
Les Artistes Steakhouse
Le Salon des Tables
Tour d'Eiffel Deux Entrance
Elevators de la Tour Eiffel & restaurant
Le Pont Alexandre III
Le Champagne Slots
Le Café Île St. Louis
● Eiffel Tower 🍴
Entrance
La Cage du Casino
MAIN CASINO
Gustav's Casino Bar
du Parc (rooftop)
Le Central Lobby Lounge
Le Paradis
Diamond Loun
Risque (2nd floor)
MAIN CASINO
Le Concierge
Lobby
Ah Sin
Le Cabaret
Diamond Check-in
Main Entrance
Taxi Service
La Reception
Show Tickets
Foy
L'Art de Paris
Valet Parking
ℹ
Entrance
LAS VEGAS BOULEVARD
ENTRANCE COURT

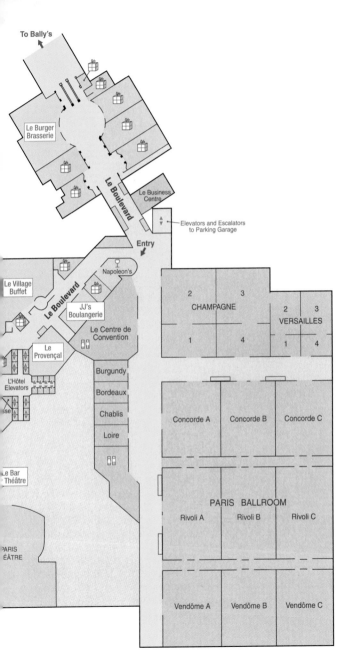

To Bally's

Le Burger
Brasserie

Le Boulevard

Le Business
Centre

Elevators and Escalators
to Parking Garage

Entry

Napoleon's

Le Village
Buffet

Le Boulevard

JJ's
Boulangerie

Le Centre de
Convention

Le
Provençal

Burgundy

Bordeaux

Chablis

Loire

L'Hôtel
Elevators

Le Bar
Théâtre

PARIS
ÉÂTRE

CHAMPAGNE

2   3

1   4

VERSAILLES

2   3

1   4

Concorde A   Concorde B   Concorde C

PARIS   BALLROOM

Rivoli A   Rivoli B   Rivoli C

Vendôme A   Vendôme B   Vendôme C

Planet Hollywood

3667 Las Vegas Blvd. S. (at Harmon Ave.)

Phone:	702-785-5555 or 877-333-9474
Fax:	702-785-5511
Web:	www.planethollywoodresort.com
Prices:	$$$

2344 Rooms
223 Suites

Unveiled in November 2007 on the site of the erstwhile Aladdin, Planet Hollywood sports a high-tech look calculated to lure a hip twenty- and thirty-something clientele. Geometric patterns and Hollywood memorabilia take shape on the casino floor under a slowly shifting kaleidoscope of colored lights and rock music.

Twin 38-story towers share the hotel's 2,600 movie-themed rooms and suites. Guests are whisked to their rooms via high-speed elevators, each with a TV on the ceiling. To keep pace with the glitterati, request a Hollywood Hip room, decked out in bold striped wallpaper and movie memorabilia. Most rooms are located near the elevators, preventing a trek down long hallways. It's also possible to access the two 6th-floor outdoor pools without having to cross the buzzing casino floor.

At dinnertime, choose Koi for Japanese cuisine or Strip House for steak *(see restaurant listing for both)*. For a casual lunch or dinner, Yolos dishes up tasty Mexican fare.

The Strip

Planet Hollywood

Where to eat…

► *RECOMMENDED*

Koi	ΧΧ	66
Strip House	ΧΧ	101
Pampas	ΧΧ	81

► *ALSO*

P.F. Chang's
Spice Market Buffet
Yolos

The Strip

Planet Hollywood

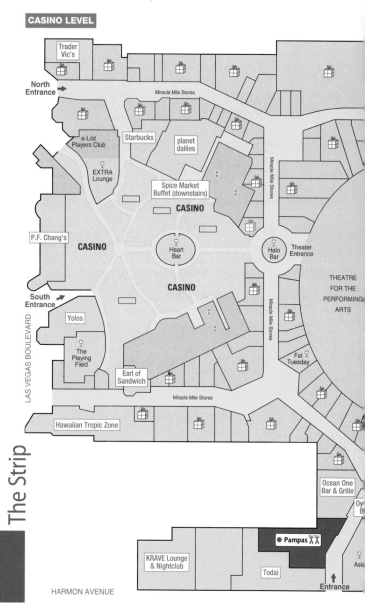

CASINO LEVEL

Trader Vic's

North Entrance

Miracle Mile Stores

a-List Players Club

Starbucks

planet dailies

EXTRA Lounge

Spice Market Buffet (downstairs)

CASINO

Miracle Mile Stores

P.F. Chang's

CASINO

Heart Bar

Halo Bar

Theater Entrance

CASINO

THEATRE FOR THE PERFORMING ARTS

South Entrance

Yolos

The Playing Field

Miracle Mile Stores

Earl of Sandwich

Fat Tuesday

Miracle Mile Stores

Hawaiian Tropic Zone

LAS VEGAS BOULEVARD

Ocean One Bar & Grille

Oy B

The Strip

● Pampas

Asi

KRAVE Lounge & Nightclub

Todai

Entrance

HARMON AVENUE

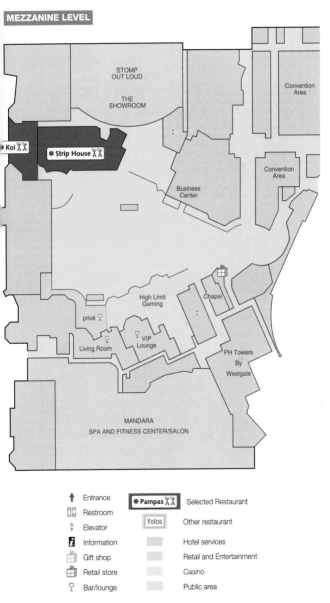

STOMP
OUT LOUD

THE
SHOWROOM

Convention
Area

● Koi 🍴

● Strip House 🍴

Business
Center

Convention
Area

High Limit
Gaming

Chapel

privé 🍷

🍷 VIP
Lounge

Living Room

PH Towers
By
Westgate

MANDARA
SPA AND FITNESS CENTER/SALON

↑	Entrance	● Pampas 🍴	Selected Restaurant
🚻	Restroom	Yolos	Other restaurant
↕	Elevator		Hotel services
🛈	Information		Retail and Entertainment
🎁	Gift shop		Casino
🎁	Retail store		Public area
🍷	Bar/lounge		

Treasure Island

 B2

3300 Las Vegas Blvd. S. (at Spring Mountain Rd.)

Phone: 702-894-7111 or 800-288-7206
Fax: 702-894-7414
Web: www.treasureisland.com
Prices: $$

2665
Rooms
220
Suites

Next door to the Mirage and now owned by the same company, Treasure Island debuted on the Strip in 1993. You'll recognize this property from the replica Mediterranean fishing village—known as Sirens' Cove—that fronts the hotel on Las Vegas Boulevard. This is the site of the steamy signature song-and-dance show, "Sirens of TI®."

A good value for the moderate price, revamped rooms and suites appeal to a fashionable crowd with their pleasing neutral tones, flat-screen TVs and roomy marble baths. In-room safes, and irons and ironing boards are included, as is high-speed Internet access (for a fee). The Elite SensaTIonal© bed provides a comfy night's sleep on its pillowtop mattress. One caveat: If you're a light sleeper, ask for a room on an upper floor, preferably one that doesn't face the Strip.

As far as entertainment goes, expect the "Mystère" to unravel at the Cirque de Soleil's surrealistic ballet without boundaries.

The Strip

Where to eat...

▶ *RECOMMENDED*

▶ *ALSO*

The Strip

Treasure Island

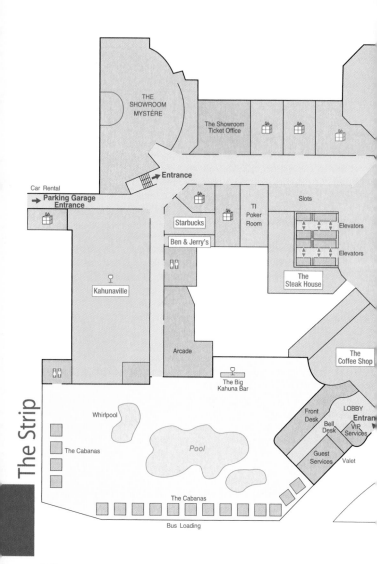

THE SHOWROOM MYSTÉRE

The Showroom Ticket Office

Car Rental

→ **Entrance**

→ **Parking Garage Entrance**

Starbucks

Ben & Jerry's

Slots

TI Poker Room

Elevators

Elevators

Kahunaville

The Steak House

Arcade

The Big Kahuna Bar

The Coffee Shop

Whirlpool

The Cabanas

Pool

Front Desk

LOBBY **Entran**

Bell Desk

VIP Services

Guest Services

Valet

The Cabanas

Bus Loading

The Strip

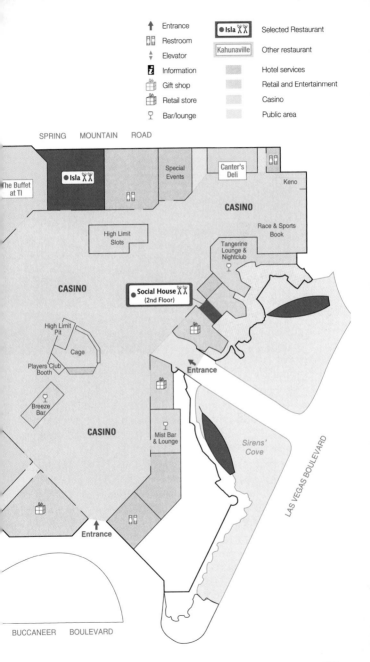

Entrance

Restroom

Elevator

Information

Gift shop

Retail store

Bar/lounge

● Isla ╳ ╳   Selected Restaurant

Kahunaville   Other restaurant

Hotel services

Retail and Entertainment

Casino

Public area

SPRING MOUNTAIN ROAD

The Buffet at TI

● Isla ╳ ╳

Special Events

Canter's Deli

Keno

CASINO

High Limit Slots

Race & Sports Book

Tangerine Lounge & Nightclub

CASINO

● Social House ╳ ╳ (2nd Floor)

Entrance

High Limit Pit

Cage

Players Club Booth

Breeze Bar

CASINO

Mist Bar & Lounge

Sirens' Cove

LAS VEGAS BOULEVARD

Entrance

BUCCANEER BOULEVARD

Venetian

3355 Las Vegas Blvd. S. (bet. Flamingo Rd. & Sands Ave.)

Phone: 702-414-1000 or 877-883-6423
Fax: 702-414-4806
Web: www.venetian.com
Prices: $$$

4027
Suites

Erected on the site of the 1952 Sands Hotel, which became the famed home of the Rat Pack, The Venetian had some big shoes to fill—and fill them it has. The sprawling resort, which recasts the Doge's Palace, the Campanile and other Venice landmarks, was launched in May 1999 for $1.5 billion.

La dolce vita envelops guests here, from the inlaid marble floors and the richly detailed frescoes on the lobby ceilings to the gondolas that float passengers through the shopping arcade on a re-creation of the Grand Canal.

More than 4,000 suites fill the property, with a staggering new tower in the works. Decked out in gold, burgundy and royal blue, "standard" suites welcome you into a marble foyer that leads into an elegant bedroom. The sunken living room with its seating area, desk, printer/fax machine and high-speed Internet access doubles as a work space—ideal for small business meetings.

Where to eat...

The Strip

Venetian

FIRST FLOOR
CASINO LEVEL

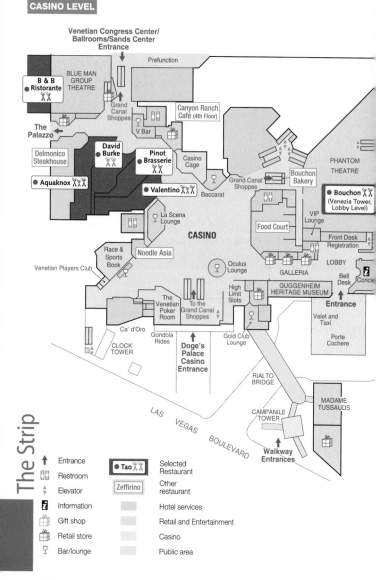

Venetian Congress Center/
Ballrooms/Sands Center
Entrance

Prefunction

BLUE MAN GROUP THEATRE

● B & B Ristorante ✗✗

Grand Canal Shoppes

Canyon Ranch Café (4th Floor)

V Bar

The Palazzo

Delmonico Steakhouse

● David Burke ✗✗

● Pinot Brasserie ✗✗

Casino Cage

PHANTOM THEATRE

Bouchon Bakery

● Aquaknox ✗✗✗

● Valentino ✗✗✗

Grand Canal Shoppes

Baccarat

● Bouchon ✗✗ (Venezia Tower, Lobby Level)

La Scena Lounge

CASINO

VIP Lounge

Food Court

Front Desk Registration

Race & Sports Book

Noodle Asia

Oculus Lounge

LOBBY

GALLERIA

Bell Desk

Concie

Venetian Players Club

The Venetian Poker Room

To the Grand Canal Shoppes

High Limit Slots

GUGGENHEIM HERITAGE MUSEUM

Entrance

Ca' d'Oro

Gondola Rides

Gold Club Lounge

Valet and Taxi

CLOCK TOWER

Doge's Palace Casino Entrance

Porte Cochere

RIALTO BRIDGE

MADAME TUSSAUDS

The Strip

LAS VEGAS BOULEVARD

CAMPANILE TOWER

Walkway Entrances

Legend

↑ Entrance	
Restroom	
↕ Elevator	
ℹ Information	
Gift shop	
Retail store	
♀ Bar/lounge	

● Tao ✗✗ Selected Restaurant

Zeffirino Other restaurant

Hotel services

Retail and Entertainment

Casino

Public area

216

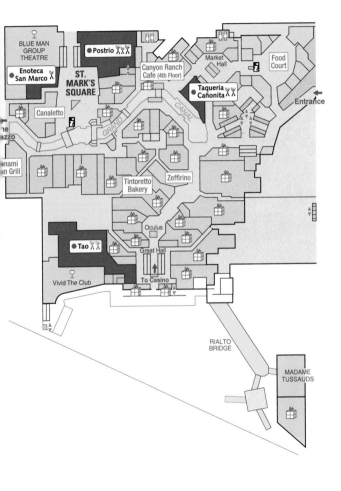

BLUE MAN GROUP THEATRE

Postrio 🍴🍴🍴

Enoteca San Marco 🍴

ST. MARK'S SQUARE

Canyon Ranch Cafe (4th Floor)

Market Hall

Food Court

Taqueria Cañonita 🍴🍴

Entrance

Canaletto

GRAND CANAL

...ne ...azzo

...nami ...an Grill

Tintoretto Bakery

Zeffirino

Oculus

Tao 🍴🍴

Great Hall

To Casino

Vivid The Club

RIALTO BRIDGE

MADAME TUSSAUDS

217

Wynn

B2

3131 Las Vegas Blvd. S. (at Sands Ave.)

Phone: 702-770-7100 or 888-320-9966
Fax: 702-770-1571
Web: www.wynnlasvegas.com
Prices: $$$$

2359
Rooms
357
Suites

What kind of a hotel can you build for $2.7 billion? To see the answer, look up the north end of the Strip to the curving bronze glass monolith named for its creator, Steve Wynn. "The man who made Las Vegas" opened this resort on the site of the old Desert Inn in April 2005. With a Tom Fazio-designed golf course, designer boutiques, and a Ferrari-Maserati dealership on-site, Wynn's posh playground leaves little to be desired.

At 640 square feet, a Resort Room here tops the "most-spacious" list. Egyptian cotton linens, a robe and slippers, a down duvet, and a pillowtop bed provide sumptuous comfort; a fax machine, three phone lines, and a flat-screen TV with Internet capability and wireless keyboard cater to business travelers. Be sure to catch a showing of the water-based spectacle Le Rêve. The show takes its name from a Picasso painting (part of Steve Wynn's art collection), which is displayed in the hotel.

Easy elegance and intimate luxury will be the hallmark of Wynn's new tower—Encore—which is scheduled to open in late 2008.

The Strip

Wynn Resorts

Where to eat…

▶ *RECOMMENDED*

Alex ❀❀	✕✕✕✕	30
Bartolotta	✕✕✕	34
The Country Club	✕✕	45
Daniel Boulud Brasserie ❀	✕✕✕	49
Okada	✕✕✕	78
Red 8	✕✕	88
Stratta	✕✕	100
SW Steakhouse	✕✕✕	105
Wing Lei ❀	✕✕✕✕	114

▶ *ALSO*

The Buffet
Chocolate
Terrace Point Café

The Strip

Wynn

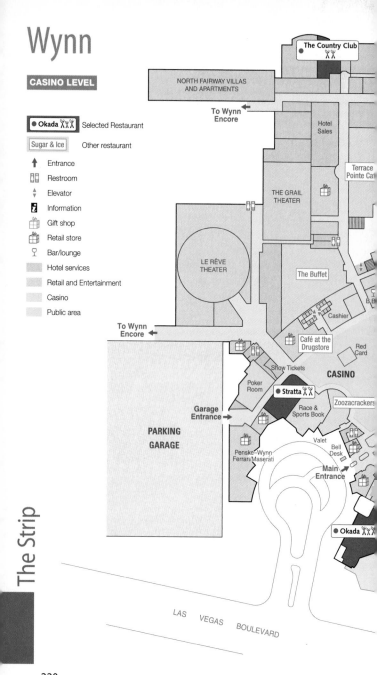

CASINO LEVEL

● Okada ✗✗✗ Selected Restaurant

Sugar & Ice Other restaurant

↑ Entrance
▯▯ Restroom
▲▼ Elevator
ℹ Information
🎁 Gift shop
🎁 Retail store
🍸 Bar/lounge
░ Hotel services
░ Retail and Entertainment
░ Casino
░ Public area

The Country Club ✗✗

NORTH FAIRWAY VILLAS AND APARTMENTS

To Wynn Encore

Hotel Sales

Terrace Pointe Ca

THE GRAIL THEATER

LE RÊVE THEATER

The Buffet

To Wynn Encore

Cashier

Café at the Drugstore

Red Card

Show Tickets

CASINO

Poker Room

● Stratta ✗✗

Zoozacrackers

Garage Entrance

Race & Sports Book

PARKING GARAGE

Valet

Bell Desk

Penske–Wynn Ferrari/Maserati

Main Entrance

● Okada ✗✗✗

The Strip

LAS VEGAS BOULEVARD

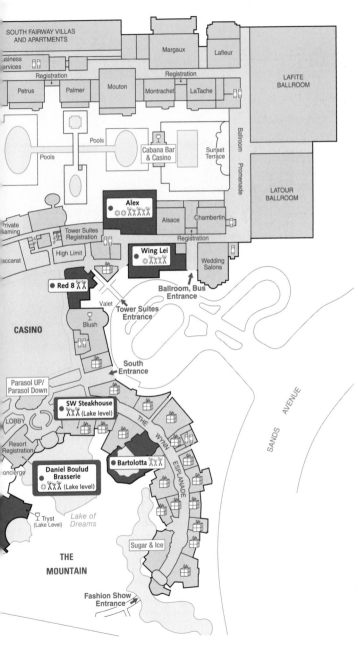

SOUTH FAIRWAY VILLAS
AND APARTMENTS

Margaux

Lafleur

Business
services

Registration

Registration

LAFITE
BALLROOM

Petrus

Palmer

Mouton

Montrachet

LaTache

Pools

Pools

Pools

Cabana Bar
& Casino

Sunset
Terrace

Ballroom Promenade

LATOUR
BALLROOM

Private
Gaming

Alex

Alsace

Chambertin

Tower Suites
Registration

High Limit

Wing Lei

Registration

Baccarat

Wedding
Salons

Red 8

Valet

Ballroom, Bus
Entrance

Tower Suites
Entrance

CASINO

Blush

South
Entrance

Parasol UP/
Parasol Down

SW Steakhouse
(Lake level)

LOBBY

THE
WYNN
ESPLANADE

Resort
Registration

Concierge

Daniel Boulud
Brasserie
(Lake level)

Bartolotta

SANDS AVENUE

Tryst
(Lake Level)

Lake of
Dreams

Sugar & Ice

THE
MOUNTAIN

Fashion Show
Entrance

Bally's

B3

3645 Las Vegas Blvd. S. (at E. Flamingo Rd.)

Phone: 702-967-4111 or 800-634-3434
Fax: N/A
Web: www.ballyslasvegas.com
Prices: $$

2549
Rooms
265
Suites

Located at the intersection of South Las Vegas Boulevard and Flamingo Avenue—known to locals as the "Four Corners"—Bally's lacks the luster of its flashy neighbors Paris and Bellagio. But given all its amenities, which include a spa and salon, a palm-lined pool, eight lighted tennis courts, nine eateries, a monorail station, and a remodeled 67,000-square-foot casino, Bally's represents good value for the price—significantly less than its fancier neighbors.

From The Strip, you access Bally's via a covered moving sidewalk. Inside, spacious attractive standard guestrooms measure 450 square feet, and all the expected comforts apply. The hotel also provides a shuttle service to and from the airport.

For classic entertainment, Donn Arden's Jubilee! re-creates a characteristic Vegas revue, complete with leggy lovelies scantily clad in bejeweled costumes and elaborate headpieces. How *do* they keep those things on?

The Strip

222

Flamingo

3555 Las Vegas Blvd. S. (at E. Flamingo Rd.)

Phone: 888-902-9929 or 800-732-2111
Fax: 702-733-3528
Web: www.flamingolasvegas.com
Prices: $$

3466
Rooms
176
Suites

In 1946 when mobster Benjamin "Bugsy" Siegel debuted his $6-million "real class joint," it was touted as the world's most luxurious hotel. Despite its desert locale, the Flamingo lured players with sterling-silver place settings and a tuxedo-clad staff.

Since then, the 105-room "House that Bugsy Built" has been transformed into a towering resort (the trap doors and tunnels that Siegel built into his suite were destroyed during the course of expansions). Deluxe rooms have standard décor, while modern "Go" rooms kick up the comfort with pillow-top mattresses, DVD/CD players, flat-screen TVs, and wireless Internet access.

The resort's centerpiece is the tropical wildlife habitat in its 15-acre "backyard." Real pink flamingos flourish in this oasis, alongside four palm-shaded pools. When the sun goes down, enjoy a ribeye at Steakhouse46, then check out singer Toni Braxton or comedian George Wallace—just a couple of the performers here.

The Strip

Luxor

B4

3900 Las Vegas Blvd. S. (at Reno Ave.)

Phone: 702-262-4444 or 888-777-0188
Fax: 702-262-4404
Web: www.luxor.com
Prices: $$

3918
Rooms
487
Suites

Walk like an Egyptian into this massive, 30-story pyramid, beneath a 110-foot-tall replica of the Sphinx. A scale model of the Great Pyramid of Giza, Luxor abounds inside with temple façades, hieroglyphic panels and murals depicting life in ancient Egypt. It's quite an impressive scene, gazing up at the interior of the structure from the Atrium level above the casino, where theaters, restaurants, and King Tut's Tomb and Museum are located.

To reach their rooms, guests board "inclinators," elevators that travel up the interior slope of the 350-foot pyramid at a 39-degree angle. Egyptian-inspired décor runs to red and gold hues, inlaid wood furnishings and pale marble. Many of the tower rooms are newly renovated.

Mandalay Place shopping mall fills a skybridge that connects Luxor to Mandalay Bay, while Nurture, the Spa at Luxor, pampers guests with treatments fit for a Pharoah.

The Strip

Monte Carlo

 B4

3770 Las Vegas Blvd. S. (bet. Harmon & Tropicana Aves.)

Phone: 702-730-7777 or 888-529-4828
Fax: 702-730-7350
Web: www.montecarlo.com
Prices: $$

2791
Rooms
211
Suites

MGM Mirage

Set back from the boulevard, the Monte Carlo flaunts an understated elegance. The ambience of Monaco surrounds you here, starting with the marble-lined lobby, dripping with crystal chandeliers and adorned with potted palms.

Cherrywood furnishings, Italian marble entryways and baths, flat-screen TVs and high-speed Internet access are some of the perks in the deluxe rooms. Suites run from 700 square feet to 825 square feet (lavish penthouse suites start at 1,800 square feet) and add amenities such as whirlpool tubs, mini-refrigerators, wet bars, in-room safes, and pull-out sofa beds.

Illusion reigns at the hotel's Lance Burton Theatre, where the master magician transforms white gloves into white doves, makes a Corvette disappear, and pulls beautiful showgirls out of a suitcase.

Dining options include formal French cuisine at André's *(see restaurant listing)*, margaritas and Mexican fare at casual Diablo's Cantina, and the new BRAND Steakhouse for meat lovers.

The Strip

Stratosphere

2000 Las Vegas Blvd. S. (bet. Sahara & St. Louis Aves.)

Phone: 702-380-7777 or 800-998-6937
Fax: 702-380-7732
Web: www.stratospherehotel.com
Prices: $

2313
Rooms
131
Suites

A landmark on the north end of Las Vegas Boulevard, Stratosphere stands at the height of Vegas spectacular. However, this hotel may not be the ideal selection for acrophobics, since its 1,149-foot-tall tower houses an indoor/outdoor observation deck affording a dizzying panorama of The Strip and the surrounding valley.

Looming 832 feet up, Top of the World restaurant will keep your nose in the air with dinner and a killer view, while the Chapel in the Clouds accommodates lofty weddings. For thrill seekers, sky-high rides Big Shot, X-Scream, and Insanity all pack one heck of an adrenaline punch!

As for the rest of this 1996 property, it's not so thrilling, but given its desirable location, the hotel does offer comfortable, clean and quiet rooms for a comparative song. Guests can choose their accommodations among those in the Regency Tower (the original tower, renovated in 2005), the World Tower, and the Premier Tower, which contains the property's largest rooms.

The Strip

Carriage House

B3

105 E. Harmon Ave. (bet. Audrie St. & Las Vegas Blvd. S.)

Phone:	702-798-1020 or 800 221 2301 ext. 65
Fax:	702-798 1020 ext. 112
Web:	www.carriagehouselasvegas.com
Prices:	$

154
Rooms

If you don't mind sacrificing a few luxuries, the Carriage House is a smart lodging choice. Staffed with courteous and helpful personnel, the tasteful hotel offers prices that will leave you with plenty of change to play the slots.

This non-gaming property makes a good alternative for families. Parents will treasure the fact that there's no casino here, and security dictates that a room key is necessary to operate the elevator. Kids will enjoy the outdoor heated pool and the illuminated tennis/basketball court. Both rooms and suites are equally comfortable for all and thoughtfully outfitted with a fully equipped kitchenette, a DVD and VCR, a hair dryer, a safe, an iron and ironing board, and complimentary high-speed Internet access. Suites come with a queen-size sofa bed in the living room to accommodate kids or even extra guests.

If it's the bustle on The Strip you crave, rest assured that the Carriage House is only a short walk away from the MGM Grand and its monorail station.

East of The Strip

Green Valley Ranch

2300 Paseo Verde Dr. (at I-215), Henderson

Phone: 702-617-7777 or 866-782-9487
Fax: 702-617-7748
Web: www.greenvalleyranchresort.com
Prices: $$

**490
Rooms**

You won't miss out on the action at Green Valley Ranch. Located 7 miles East of The Strip via I-215, this Mediterranean-style resort has it all: a casino, a 10,000-square-foot European day spa, a cinema complex, even a working vineyard.

Nearly 500 spacious rooms, made plush by down comforters, luxurious linens and feather beds, are divided between the East and West towers. Dark wood furnishings uphold the ritzy feel, while large windows look out over the surrounding mountains.

In front of the hotel stretches a "Main Street" of shops and restaurants; the "backyard" holds an 8-acre pool complex with a sand beach. Restaurant options cater to carnivores, between Hank's Fine Steak & Martinis and nearby Lucille's Smokehouse Barbeque *(see restaurant listing for both)*. For entertainment, you can dance the night away at the hip Whiskey Bar.

The resort provides shuttle service to and from McCarran International Airport and The Strip.

East of The Strip

Hard Rock

B3

4455 Paradise Rd. (at Harmon Ave.)

Phone: 702-693-5000 or 800-473-7625
Fax: 702-693-5588
Web: www.hardrockhotel.com
Prices: $$

583
Rooms
63
Suites

♿

Leave the kids—and your parents—at home if you're planning to stay at the Hard Rock. Chances are that neither will appreciate the blaring rock music or the raucous adult pool scene where many of the things that stay in Vegas happen. Twenty-somethings, however, get their groove on at Body English, The Joint, and the newest club, Wasted Space, where top rock-music acts perform.

Outfitted with sleek lines, flat-screen plasma TVs, and French doors that actually open, rooms are designed with everyone from rock stars to roadies in mind. Of course, the glitterati go for the 1,300-square-foot Celebrity Suites, where they can kick back in high style. Expect to see some heavenly bodies at the Beach Club, lounging in private cabanas or trying their luck at swim-up blackjack.

Plans are in full swing to rock on with more than 900 new guest rooms, a convention center, a bigger casino, and a new spa. Keep in mind that construction noise could be an issue until the expansion is complete later in 2009.

East of The Strip

Hilton

 B-C2

3000 Paradise Rd. (bet. Convention Center Dr. & Karen Ave.)

Phone: 702-732-5111 or 888-737-7117
Fax: 702-732-5778
Web: www.lvhilton.com
Prices: $$

2833
Rooms
124
Suites

Las Vegas Hilton

Convenient to the Las Vegas Convention Center, the Hilton claims the distinction of having hosted Elvis Presley's Sin City debut in July 1969 (though the hotel was then known as the International). Elvis may have left the building, but his legend lives on in the bronze statue recently reinstalled in the hotel. Today other entertainment legends hold sway here, notably Barry Manilow, who is headlining through 2008 at the 1,700-seat Hilton Theater.

Vegas glitz is in short supply in this off-the-Strip property. Rooms are basic and conservative in decoration, and you won't find the type of service you'd be treated to at a swankier Strip hotel. Even so, the Hilton has some nice amenities—a large outdoor pool, a fitness center and spa, a salon, even a putting green and a video arcade—for the price. Trekkies will love the virtual-reality ride, Star Trek: The Experience.

East of The Strip

Loews Lake Las Vegas

101 Montelago Blvd. (off Lake Mead Pkwy.), Henderson

Phone: 702-567-6000 or 800-235-6397
Fax: 702-567-6067
Web: www.loewshotels.com
Prices: $$$

447
Rooms
46
Suites

Loews Hotels

Forget about gambling, head east, and place your bets on Loews instead. Sure, there's no casino here, but Loews nevertheless holds a full house when it comes to location. Once you look out on the lovely waters of Lake Las Vegas with the rugged peaks in the distance, you won't miss the neon and the crowds at all.

Service is gracious and the guestrooms are comfortably outfitted with all the modern amenities: cotton linens, terry robes, flat-screen TVs, in-room video games, and a safe that will accommodate your laptop. For the best water panorama, book a premium lake view or a grand luxury king room. And don't leave the kids or the pets at home; both are welcome at Loews.

A spa, two pools, and access to two championship golf courses as well as lake watersports mean that you'll find plenty to fill your time here. For fine dining, Marssa *(see restaurant listing)* adds a taste of the Pacific Rim to the hotel's colorful Moroccan theme.

East of The Strip

Platinum

B3

211 E. Flamingo Rd. (at Koval Ln.)

Phone:	702-365-5000 or 877-211-9211
Fax:	702-365-5000
Web:	www.theplatinumhotel.com
Prices:	$$

255
Suites

Pick the Platinum for a subdued, more residential off-Strip experience. This non-gaming, all-suite property shines with a full range of services and amenities, including an indoor/outdoor pool with a spacious sundeck, a state-of-the-art fitness center, a noteworthy restaurant called Kilawat *(see restaurant listing)*, and the 4,000-square-foot WELL spa.

Showing off earthy shades of brown, beige, and cream, each comfortable one- and two-bedroom suite hits the mother lode with high-speed Internet access (both wired and wireless) and a full kitchen, well-appointed with dishes, glassware, cutlery, and stainless-steel appliances. Bedrooms provide feather beds, robes, and plenty of closet space. Just off the living room, a spacious patio includes seating for four. Princess and Marquise suites add fireplaces and washer/dryers.

Expect the service to be friendly, but unobtrusive. And when you're itching for more action, all the glitz and gambling of The Strip is less than two blocks away.

East of The Strip

Ritz-Carlton Lake Las Vegas

G3

1610 Lake Las Vegas Pkwy. (off Lake Mead Pkwy.), Henderson

Phone:	702-567-4700 or 800-241-3333
Fax:	702-567-4777
Web:	www.ritz-carlton.com
Prices:	$$$

314
Rooms
35
Suites

Location, location, location. These are the three best reasons to stay at the Ritz-Carlton Lake Las Vegas. A mere 17-mile drive East of The Strip brings you to this serene oasis, arranged on the shore of a 320-acre privately owned lake. The resort's architecture recalls the towns of Tuscany—and even spans the water with a replica of the Ponte Vecchio in Florence.

Attentive, personalized service is the signature of the Ritz. Guests are addressed by name and every effort is made to ensure a memorable stay. Standard rooms belie their name, feathering these nests with warm pastels, Frette linens, and Bulgari amenities in the baths (hint: request a room with a balcony). Business travelers enjoy desks with high-speed Internet access and ample room for laptops.

The boutiques and cafes of MonteLago Village are accessible right outside the hotel. Guests stay busy between the fitness center, golf, and water sports; while the spa, the pool, and the white-sand beach offer more than enough opportunities to relax.

East of The Strip

Westin Casuarina

B3

160 E. Flamingo Rd. (at Koval Ln.)

Phone: 702-836-5900
Fax: 702-836-9776
Web: www.starwoodhotels.com
Prices: $$

816
Rooms
10
Suites

With a modest 825 rooms and suites, the Westin Casuarina is absolutely intimate compared to its sprawling neighbors on The Strip. There's no on-site shopping (the Forum Shops and Fashion Show Mall are just a half-mile away), but you will have access to a concierge, a well-equipped fitness facility (open 24/7), the state-of-the-art Hibiscus Spa, and covered parking. The hotel caters to business travelers with 25,000 square feet of meeting space, complete with high-speed Internet access and video-conferencing capabilities.

Warm woods, sleek lines, and earth-tone palettes fill the rooms, which start at 370-square-foot traditional accommodations and move up from there to deluxe one- or two- bedroom suites. No matter the level of luxury, all rooms come with dual showerheads, coffeemakers with Starbucks coffee, in-room safes, fluffy towels and robes, and Westin's Heavenly Bed® with its 10-layer pillowtop mattress. Pets are welcome here.

East of The Strip

JW Marriott Resort

 D1

221 N. Rampart Blvd. (off Summerlin Pkwy.)

Phone:	702-869-7777 or 877-869-8777
Fax:	702-869-7339
Web:	www.jwlasvegasresort.com
Prices:	**$$**

469
Rooms
79
Suites

Targeting tranquility, this sprawling Spanish Revival-style resort seems worlds away from The Strip. Although the Marriott is only a 20-minute drive northwest of Las Vegas Boulevard, serenity reigns in the views of the striated mountains that abound from this 54-acre property in Summerlin.

Ignoring the temptations of the casino, golf enthusiasts come here to play at one of the 11 courses nearby (the staff will gladly reserve you a tee time). Then, of course, there's the 40,000-square-foot Aquae Sulis Spa, where your concerns will melt away during a Thai massage or a wild lavender body wrap.

Divided between the Spa Tower and the Palms Tower, guest rooms are tastefully decorated in warm shades of beige. Feather beds, walk-in closets, whirlpool tubs, and separate rain showers are a few of the frills. Eight eateries here run the gamut from American (Ceres) to pub grub (J.C. Wooloughan; *see restaurant listing*) to sushi at Shizen (*see restaurant listing*).

West of The Strip

Orleans

4500 W. Tropicana Ave. (at Arville St.)

Phone: 702-365-7111 or 800-675-3267
Fax: 702-365-7500
Web: www.orleanscasino.com
Prices: $

1867
Rooms
19
Suites

With its French Quarter theme, the Orleans hotel offers a variety of action, including a casino, a 70-lane bowling center, and an 18-screen movie theater. Then there's the 9,000-seat Orleans Arena next door, which hosts everything from monster truck rallies to championship basketball tournaments. In the hotel's showroom, you can catch big-name music acts (Gladys Knight, Etta James, Air Supply) and comedians (George Carlin, Don Rickles, Steven Wright).

Comfortable, quiet, and well-maintained rooms— or "petite suites" as the hotel bills them—don't skimp on size at 450 square feet as the standard. Complimentary valet parking and free shuttle service to The Strip are provided, along with 40,000 square feet of meeting space and 11 eateries, ranging from Subway and T.G.I. Fridays for the basics to Canal Street and the Prime Rib Loft for more upscale fare.

And if you just want to kick back, head for the spa or the pool, and let the good times roll.

West of The Strip

Palms

A3

4321 W. Flamingo Rd. (at Wynn Rd.)

Phone:	702-942-7777 or 866-942-7777
Fax:	702-942-7001
Web:	www.palms.com
Prices:	$$

573
Rooms
147
Suites

The young and the hip party at the Palms, where the night never ends between the exclusive Playboy Club with its high-stakes gaming and "bunny" dealers; Rain's raised dance floor; Ghostbar's indoor/outdoor lounge; and Moon, with its retractable penthouse roof. Music-industry VIPs can even mix their own CDs in the hotel's private recording studio.

Guests may spend limited time in their rooms, but when they do, they can count on light-filled, contemporary quarters chock-a-block with upscale amenities. Suites on the Fantasy Tower's Party Floor feature the likes of a pool table, a DJ booth, bowling lanes, and an indoor basketball court. Expect "service on the spot" at the touch of a button on your room phone.

Opened in spring 2008, Palms Place condo hotel grabs the glitterati with a mix of fully furnished studio units, one-bedroom suites, and lavish penthouses. It connects to the Palms casino via an enclosed motorized walkway.

West of The Strip

Red Rock Resort

11011 W. Charleston Blvd. (at I-215)

Phone:	702-797-7777 or 866-767-7773
Fax:	702-797-7831
Web:	www.redrocklasvegas.com
Prices:	$$$

814
Rooms
45
Suites

Dripping with crystal chandeliers and lined with onyx, the lobby of the Red Rock Resort envelops visitors in a stunningly bold design whose earth tones mimic the hues of the nearby Red Rock mountains.

The rooms are spacious, elegant cocoons done in shades of deep brown with accents of rust red and willow green. Starting at 525 square feet, standard accommodations boast a Bose sound system, floor-to-ceiling windows framing red-rock panoramas, high-speed Internet access, and a phone equipped for video conferencing. A range of suites epitomize luxury.

Amenities include a nightclub, a spa, and the three-acre "backyard," where you can lounge at the pool while attendants cater to your every whim. Hachi joined the restaurant collection here in summer 2007, and serves up a medley of Japanese fare. For the restless, there's a 72-lane bowling center, a fitness center, and customized hiking, rock-climbing and biking trips in the mountains.

West of The Strip

Rio

3700 W. Flamingo Rd. (at Valley View Blvd.)

Phone: 702-777-7777 or 866-746-7671
Fax: 702-777-6462
Web: www.riolasvegas.com
Prices: $$

2563
Suites

Infused with the sights and sounds of Brazil's *Carnivale*, the Rio rocks from its 100,000 square feet of gaming space to the *Masquerade Show in the Sky*, a raucous music and dance show performed atop floats suspended from the ceiling above the casino floor.

A one-stop entertainment destination, the hotel hosts the interactive production *Tony n' Tina's Wedding* and the macabre comedy of Penn and Teller—not to mention the Chippendales' hunky all-male revue. By day you can take the whole family bowling at Lucky Strike Lanes; by night this venue does an adult twist with DJ music and a hip bar scene. The party wags on with poolside blackjack, flair bartenders, and four pools at VooDoo Beach, while McFadden's Saloon goes wild with fishbowl cocktails and bartop dancing.

Every room is a suite here. All are outfitted with floor-to-ceiling windows, refrigerators, and safes. Upgraded rooms sport amenities such as wet bars, jacuzzis, and dedicated concierge service.

West of The Strip

Trump International
Hotel & Tower

B2

2000 Fashion Show Mall Dr.
(bet. Industrial Rd. & Las Vegas Blvd. S.)

Phone: 702-982-0000 or 866-646-8164
Fax: 702-476-8450
Web: www.trumplasvegashotel.com
Prices: $$$$

1282
Suites

It was just a matter of time before The Donald got in on the high-rolling action in Vegas. Opened just West of The Strip (adjacent to Fashion Show Mall) in April 2008, the Trump International Hotel pays tribute to its namesake with sumptuous suites, impeccable service, and contemporary American cuisine at DJT restaurant *(see restaurant listing)*.

A stay in the 64-story tower, wrapped in 24-carat gold glass, begins with a greeting from white-gloved doormen. Even the smallest suites are a study in luxury, their fully equipped kitchens featuring a stainless-steel Sub-Zero refrigerator, a Wolf stovetop, and Bosch appliances. When you're not relaxing in your room, the pampering spa and state-of-the-art health club will keep you in top shape.

Service here speaks for itself. Valets place chilled bottles of water in your car; a tray of truffles and bottled water is presented at turndown; and the signature Trump Attaché service ensures that your every need will be seen to 24 hours a day.

Golden Nugget

129 Fremont St. (at 1st St.)

Phone: 702-385-7111 or 800-846-5336
Fax: 702-386-8362
Web: www.goldennugget.com
Prices: $

1874
Rooms
33
Suites

Named for the 61-pound, 11-ounce chunk of gold displayed in a quiet corner of the lobby, the Golden Nugget was the first casino on Fremont Street. The hotel, which opened in 1946, still exudes the spirit of old Las Vegas without appearing antiquated. Thank the recent $170-million renovation, which rejuvenated this aging matron in just over a year.

A new 600-seat showroom books performers like Rich Little, while the refreshed spa houses a salon and fitness center. Unveiled in December 2007, The Grand is a multipurpose event and conference center. More recent additions include an expanded gaming floor, a new sushi restaurant, and Gold Diggers nightclub.

Surprisingly large renovated rooms in the two towers all have high-speed Internet access. Downstairs, the pool has been transformed into a tropical oasis centering on The Tank, where you can swim nose-to-snout with beady-eyed sharks, separated only by a few inches of glass.

Downtown

Main Street Station

200 N. Main St. (at Stewart Ave.)

Phone:	702-387-1896 or 800-465-0711
Fax:	702-386-4466
Web:	www.mainstreetcasino.com
Prices:	$

406
Rooms
14
Suites

This Victorian-style casino cashes in on the ambience of late-19th-century San Francisco with its mahogany wall paneling, stained-glass skylights, and period antiques. Located just a few blocks from the computer-generated sound-and-light show known as the Fremont Street Experience, Main Street Station provides a respite from Downtown's flash and dash.

Pick up a brochure at the front desk and take a self-guided tour of the property's noteworthy antiques. Along the way you'll discover Louisa May Alcott's private Pullman railcar, a fireplace from Prestwick Castle in Scotland, and even a piece of the Berlin Wall, albeit in the men's room, off the main casino floor!

By contrast, guestrooms are contemporary in style, with dark armoires, cushioned armchairs, and plantation shutters. The clientele of older couples, tour groups, and families don't seem to mind that there's no in-room dining; Triple 7, one of three on-site eateries, is open daily from 11:00 A.M. until 7:00 P.M.

Downtown

Notes